ENDORSEMENTS

"Demons are real. The Devil is real. But Deliverance is also real! As a pastor, I am often asked about demonic activity. While there are countless resources on supernatural activity, I've never run across one that is so consumed with biblical insights providing such practical tools as my friend Steve Hemphill has done with *What Are The Stakes?*"

Pastor Glynn Stone, PhD,
Mobberly Baptist Church, Longview, TX.

"Steve Hemphill is a driver. He wants great things for us. *What Are The Stakes?* will direct one's focus to become more attentive to the mighty things God can do."

Terry Rush, Senior Minister,
Memorial Drive Church of Christ, Tulsa, OK.

"C.S. Lewis wisely counseled that we avoid two dangers with regard to Satan: giving him too much credit and giving him too little. Steve Hemphill helps us avoid the latter through engaging anecdotes and Biblical discussion. May it prompt all of us to delve deeper as we seek to glorify Jesus!"

Dr. David English, Executive Pastor,
First Baptist Church, Longview, TX.

"There are big-time pastors who have told me they will not touch this topic because of the literal hell it will bring down on them and their families. Steve Hemphill has the courage to expose evil for what it is. For twenty-five years I've watched him change the world as a warrior for Christ. This book is his best weapon yet."

Billy E. Hibbs, Chairman/CEO Heartland
Security Insurance Group, Tyler, TX.

"Steve Hemphill exposes the truth here: that Satan is indeed real! In a simple and direct fashion Steve reveals the devil's schemes and tactics that can lead to confusion and control. Steve writes with a two-fold purpose: To affirm that the devil and his passion to deceive are real, and to point to the source of hope and freedom: Jesus. Steve writes from a heart of compassion and a genuine love for people. Thank you, Steve!"

Jackie L. Chesnutt,
Southside Church of Christ, Rogers, AR.

"Steve Hemphill loves God's word. He has courageously chosen to study and teach important Biblical concepts that few Christians have been bold enough to pursue. We don't like to talk about Satan or his powers, or the fact that without God and the presence of His Holy Spirit, we are powerless against him! For all who have heard Steve speak, a chord has been struck, and they have been moved to share their encounters with the power of evil in their own lives. In this new book, you will read about the experiences of many who have sought to rid their lives of Satan's evil influence. You will see how Christians can be triumphant!"

Chuck Duvall, Longview, TX.

"Every day we see the fruits of evil. With the testimony of a multitude of witnesses, Steve's book is a shaking reminder that a real spiritual war is raging all around us. He reminds us of the weapons God has given us to be victorious. It's time we become effective on the battlefield."

Ron Hutchison, Longview, TX.

BIO

Steve Hemphill is now in full-time ministry after 30 years in the business world. He's written four books including "My Search for the Real Heaven" and "My Search for Prayers Satan Hates." His true love is speaking, telling his amazing God stories everywhere he goes. Invite him to your church for a series or an outreach. You'll never be the same. Visit his web sites @ PrayerThoughts.com and HopeHelpHealing.com. His on line schedule is available there along with thousands of free PowerPoint slides for use in your church, Bible class, or small group.

What are the Stakes?

What are the Stakes?

GOD MARKERS ON THE LAND

STEVE HEMPHILL

TATE PUBLISHING
AND ENTERPRISES, LLC

This book is designed to provide accurate and authoritative information with regard to the subject matter covered. This information is given with the understanding that neither the author nor Tate Publishing, LLC is engaged in rendering legal, professional advice. Since the details of your situation are fact dependent, you should additionally seek the services of a competent professional.

The opinions expressed by the author are not necessarily those of Tate Publishing, LLC.

Published by Tate Publishing & Enterprises, LLC
127 E. Trade Center Terrace | Mustang, Oklahoma 73064 USA
1.888.361.9473 | www.tatepublishing.com

Tate Publishing is committed to excellence in the publishing industry. The company reflects the philosophy established by the founders, based on Psalm 68:11,

"The Lord gave the word and great was the company of those who published it."

Book design copyright © 2016 by Tate Publishing, LLC. All rights reserved.
Cover design by Samson Lim
Interior design by Manolito Bastasa

Published in the United States of America

ISBN: 978-1-68270-532-2
1. Religion / Demonology & Satanism
2. Religion / Theology
15.12.14

The Invisible War

> And the last enemy to be destroyed is death. (1 Cor. 15:26, NLT)

THERE IS AN invisible war going on. It's a life-and-death struggle. But most are totally unaware.

Pretend I'm an Alabama football fan. It's noon. It's game day. It's time for the kickoff. But as you grab your drink and snack to enjoy the kickoff, you see something strange on your seventy-inch ultrahigh-definition television: the team is lazily walking out on the field in shorts and tennis shoes, strolling toward midfield, carrying bags with their equipment. Their helmets and shoulder pads are still in the bags. They throw the bags down and start...what are they doing? Making sandwiches?

The opposing team is lined up to kick off, but your 'Bama heroes are passing the mustard and chips to each other. You can't believe your eyes. Your mouth is open, and your heart skips a beat.

The whistle blows to signal the opposing kicker it's time to start. You panic. The other team races down the field after the ball, running over your heroes, knocking them down, causing injury and insult.

Three Alabama players had the sense to be suited up and ready, but the rest of the team is oblivious to the opposition's preparedness and strategies. Many are moaning and rolling around on the turf in pain, screaming for help and angry at their own coach. They shout obscenities at the very ones who were supposed to have them ready for this day. But the 'Bama coaches are also getting run over and hurt.

One Alabama player catches the ball, and two others try to block for him, but there are just too many. He gets hit hard, the ball pops out, and the opposition scoops it up and runs it in for a touchdown.

'Bama players shake their heads and walk around in a daze. "We're a good team," they scream. "How could this happen to us? Why do bad things happen to good people?"

Did they suit up? Did they put on their helmet of salvation, breastplate of righteousness, shoes of peace, belt of truth, shield of faith, and take up the sword of truth?

If you don't suit up for the battle and get in position and know your weapons, you're bound to lose—and get hurt in the process.

Christians are in the most important war of their lives. And, sadly, many aren't even aware of the usefulness of the armor, much less donning it every day with purpose.

You are in this war. Have you suited up? Have you read Ephesians 6 lately? Can you quote any scripture to the enemy when temptation comes your way, like Jesus did when Satan tempted Him?

This war is all about where you and your loved ones will spend eternity. Prayer matters. The words you speak every day can make a difference in your own destiny as well as the destiny of those all around you. Make them count.

Lord, open my eyes to the unseen war going on all around me. Help me to know what to say and what to do to defeat the enemies who are after me. In Jesus's name, amen.

The Beginning of the End

> Therefore you shall *keep My commandments*, and perform them: I am the Lord. (Lev. 22:31, NKJV)

The third chapter of the book of 2 Timothy describes what it will be like in the End Times. It's quite telling. As I read through the prevalent qualities, I realized how alarming it was that so many of these could be seen in abundance today. But the one it leads up to in the fifth verse scared me the most. Let me explain.

The first verse says that the End Times will be hard times:

> "You should know this, Timothy, that *in the last days there will be very difficult times.*" (2 Tim. 3:1, NLT)

The first part of the second verse says that people will only love themselves and be consumed with their money:

> *People will love* only *themselves and* their *money.* (2 Tim. 3:2, NLT)

It goes on to say that End Times folks will brag, scoff at God, disobey their parents, act ungrateful, and trample on the sacred:

> They will be *boastful* and *proud, scoffing at God, disobedient* to their parents, and *ungrateful.* They will *consider nothing sacred.* (2 Tim. 3:2, NLT)

The third verse reveals that End Times people will be mean, out of control, and have a cruel hatred for goodness:

> They will *be unloving and unforgiving*; they will *slander* others and have *no self-control*. They will be *cruel and hate what is good*. (2 Tim. 3:3, NLT)

Verse 4 goes on to say that they will be reckless and betray their friends, they will be puffed up with pride, and they will be in love with pleasure:

> They will *betray their friends*, be *reckless*, be puffed up with *pride, and love pleasure* rather than God. (2 Tim. 3:4, NLT)

Now here's the really scary part:

> *They will act religious*, but *they will reject the power* that could make them godly. (2 Tim. 3:5, NLT)

They will act religious. They will be churchgoers. They will be regular attenders. They might even be part of the leadership or the church staff.

You know, you're not a chicken just because you sit in a chicken house. And you're not a Christian just because you sit in a church. There are wolves in sheep's clothing. There are predators among the believers. And they aren't easy to spot. But here's a hint, a clue that will help you spot them: they will deny the power of God.

I want to tell you right now at the start of this book: God is not the great "I Used to Could." He is the "I Am." That is a continuing action version of that verb. God always has, and God still can, and God still does. God's Holy Spirit came when Jesus left, and God is still at work in this world, drawing men to Himself (John 6:44). Don't ever forget that.

Notice also from 2 Timothy 3:5 that God's power makes us godly. So denying God's power makes men ungodly. Plain and simple.

I mention this now, because it's going to take faith to receive the amazing stories I'm about to share with you in this book. So here's a verse you need to be reminded of before we can begin:

> Because they did not have faith, he did not perform many miracles there. (Matt. 13:58, GNT)

From the lips of our Lord Himself, lack of faith limits God's miraculous power. There. I said it. Sorry if that's hard for you to take. It was for me, but it's a biblical truth I must learn to accept.

Jesus's miracles were limited to people who had the faith it takes to receive them. Little faith means few (if any) miracles. Great faith has the potential for many and great miracles. Faith and miracles are connected. Your lack of faith limits God's miraculous power in your life. In summary, miracles require faith.

The Lord's Supper is an act of faith. What is the Lord's Supper for? It's a fellowship meal and a connection to the living God. It's a symbol of your covenant relationship with God. It's also a reminder of the resurrection of Jesus Christ, of the blood he shed on your behalf. Perhaps most importantly it's an admission of an unseen realm and a connection to that realm.

Prayer is also an act of worship. Prayer expresses a need to a God who can do something about it; it connects us to Him. Prayer changes the future. If you don't believe that—don't pray. So prayer is also an admission of an unseen realm.

This leads me to my definition for the term: spiritual warfare.

Spiritual Warfare = Things happening in our physical world because of the actions of spiritual forces in the unseen realm.

And make no mistake, *prayer affects those unseen forces.* Every day and in every way.

The last short story in my first book was called "The Atheist at Burger King." (If you need to be reminded of the entire story, refer to the appendix at the back of this book.)

Just as an overview reminder: I had noticed some New Testament passages—including 1 Corinthians 12:3—that revealed that non-Christians can't say the words, "Jesus Is Lord." Only those with the Holy Spirit (Christians) are able to vocalize that statement. I have tested this biblical truth many times since discovering it, and so far I've found it to be true. Some literally cannot say the words, "Jesus is Lord." Because He isn't their Lord. A few of the ones I asked actually got visibly angry and combative when asked if Jesus is Lord. Some screamed and cursed. Really.

Lord, the world seems darker and more evil every day. Help me to remember that when the world is the darkest, the church can shine the brightest. As we near the end of the age and I see the things You predicted in the world around me, help me to remember that I don't work for the president. I work for You— the King of all kings and Lord of all lords—and You know how to take care of Your own.

Jesus Is the **Only** Way to God

> Jesus said to him, "I am the way, and the truth, and the life. *No one comes to the Father except through me.*"
> (John 14:6, ESV)

Jesus is the operative word. "Jesus" is offensive. Using this word makes you a bigot, narrow-minded, and offensively exclusive. It's the word the world does not want you to use in a way—especially at the end of a prayer.

The world doesn't mind if you pray to any "god." They just refuse to listen if you invoke the name of Jesus. Have you ever wondered why? John 14:6 is the reason. Jesus claimed to be the only way to God. Because He is. This is a faith issue. You either believe it, or you don't. This is offensive to the Buddhist, Hindu, and many other sects, and especially to Arabs. It offends them because if that is really true, then all those without Jesus will be left outside the gates of a joyful eternity with God.

Is it true? As stated above, this is emphatically stated by the mouth of Jesus. As C. S. Lewis pointed out, this doesn't leave you the option of calling Jesus a good man or a prophet. He's either lying or crazy or God's Son. Who is He to you? I'll tell you who he is to me: He is my Savior, the promised Messiah, and He's also my Lord and Master. And He's either all that to you too, or He's nothing at all. He doesn't accept half-hearted commitments. You can't be baptized and hold one hand out of the water. God doesn't accept applications, just wholehearted commitments to His one and only Son. Get the picture. Jesus is the only way to God.

Lord, use my life and my witness to help expand the borders of Your Kingdom. In Jesus's name, amen.

The Enemy Hates the Name of Jesus

> The man shouted in a loud voice, *"What do you want with me, Jesus, Son of the Most High God? I command you in God's name not to torture me!"* (Mark 5:7, NCV)

Several churches in my city combined their resources many years ago to create a local, nondenominational outreach to help the underprivileged. It's called "Caring and Sharing." They serve over one thousand families per month primarily with food and clothing. Many volunteers from several local groups are involved with helping on a regular basis.

One day there was a problem with one of the applicants. This woman was anxious and quite upset, so much so that she starting yelling and causing a commotion. Some of the volunteers who were nearby tried to jump in and help, working to calm her. But it wasn't helping.

One of the volunteers was a good friend of mine. She quickly came to try and calm the situation, dismissing the other workers and taking over. She talked quietly and softly as they were seated, assuring the woman that she would be served as quickly as possible. It began to work. Everything was improving until she said something that upset the lady.

"We love you," she intoned. "We are going to make sure you are helped."

The woman got quiet, nodding and settling down markedly. "And Jesus loves you," she continued.

At the name of Jesus, the woman went crazy. She jerked her head away, quickly yelling and screaming, "No."

At first the worker didn't make the connection. She had been making progress until something had set the woman off. What was it?

The worker's gentle calming voice again assured this woman that she would be taken care of.

"We love you," she said again, "and Jesus loves you."

It was the same automatic, frantic response from the woman in need. She screamed and yelled and moved away, waving her arms in frustration.

That was it. The name of Jesus is offensive to people who have a demon.

The volunteer went on to tell me that she felt sure this woman was possessed. "It was almost like foaming at the mouth," she explained. "It was that wild."

> A man out of the crowd answered, "Teacher, *I brought my mute son, made speechless by a demon*, to you. Whenever it seizes him, *it throws him to the ground. He foams at the mouth*, grinds his teeth, and goes stiff as a board. I told your disciples, hoping they could deliver him, but they couldn't." (Mark 9:17–18, The Message)

Lord, deliver me from evil, but help me to help deliver others from evil, too. Many are possessed and need Your divine intervention. Tell me what to say and teach me what to do. In Jesus's name, amen.

Bible-based thoughts based on this event: demons absolutely hate the name of Jesus Christ.

"Used-to-be" Disciples

He went up on a mountain, and *when He was seated His disciples came to Him.* (Matt. 5:1, NKJV)

The disciples of Jesus followed Him, learned from Him, and ultimately believed in Him as the Son of God. This also means they believed what He said about how to get to the Father:

Jesus answered, "I am the way, the truth, and the life. *The only way to the Father is through me."* (John 14:6, ERV)

This is a faith issue. We either believe it, or we don't. One of the things I always point out when I help with an outreach for a local congregation is this:

Just because you're in a chicken house doesn't mean you're a chicken.

And just because you're in a church house doesn't mean you're a Christian.

Association with Christians doesn't automatically make you one—although it helps nudge you that direction.

Similarly, having a title over your worship center that indicates you are a disciple of Jesus Christ doesn't necessarily mean you are. This was a lesson I was forced to learn by experience. Let me explain.

A regional denominational group invited me to speak for their annual renewal retreat in a lovely country setting. I arrived on Friday afternoon and was scheduled to speak on Friday evening and Saturday morning. Everyone was to return home on Saturday afternoon to their respective congregations, since they were all active leaders and ministers who needed to be back for Sunday worship. There were about forty men in attendance. The regional director also came to give a short presentation Friday night before I did my part.

As I often do, I opened up the floor for questions and answers at the conclusion of my first presentation. This led to a question I had never been asked in a setting like this: "What about other religions?"

"Well," I began thoughtfully, "anyone who can say, 'Jesus Is Lord,' is on the same team with us. But if they can't begin with that simple statement, they're not."

At this, the regional director (who was sitting on the second row) jumped up.

"Let me help you answer that question," she began as I retreated to the side and gave her the floor. "I have a PhD in theology, and I also took a class in world religions at _____ University, and I would never say you had to believe in Jesus to go to heaven. There are lots of ways to heaven: Buddhism, Hinduism, and many others."

Did I just hear her say that? I thought to myself. *Surely not. And if I did, surely someone would object to that biblically.*

But they didn't.

Shocked, I returned to center stage. And I felt compelled to stand for the truth of God.

"Well," I started, slowly and precisely, "Jesus said He was the only way to God, so you're not arguing with me. You're arguing with Jesus. Are there any other questions?" I continued.

The questions covered a variety of things, and things went well following all that. But I was nervous to end the session and face the lady I had just contradicted so emphatically.

After a final prayer, she rushed to the front where I was packing up my equipment.

Here it comes, I thought.

She grabbed my hand and shook it enthusiastically. "Thank you for coming," she exclaimed. "You are a gifted speaker." Then she turned and left.

What just happened? I thought. My public criticism of her position went right over her head.

> They will look and look, but they will not learn. They will listen and listen, but they will not understand. If they did learn and understand, they would come back to me and be forgiven. (Mark 4:12, NCV)

Lord, help me to be a true disciple. Help me to have the faith it takes to trust You and Your commands completely. In Jesus's name, amen.

Bible-Based Thoughts Based on this Event:

Demons want you completely blind to the truth of Scripture. Demons want you to think there are lots of ways to God besides Jesus.

Words Have Power

> God said, "Let there be light," and there was light. (Gen. 1:3, NLT)

What if I walked in to your house and said, "Watch this: S-T-O-O-L!" and a real stool appeared right in front of you. You could pick it up and hold it, you could sit on it, and you could see that it was permanent and tangible. What would you tell your friends? You would say, "Wow! That Steve Hemphill is something! He just spoke the word *stool*, and one appeared out of thin air! A real one!"

God did that with the earth. And the sun. And all the planets and stars. That's the power of the God of the universe, the Father of Jesus.

> I will give you the keys of the kingdom of heaven, and *whatever you bind on earth will be bound in heaven, and whatever you loose on earth will be loosed in heaven.* (Matt. 16:19, NKJV)

Christians are children of God, part of the royal family, coheirs with Jesus of the eternal blessings that will come to all who are part of His family. Once you name Jesus as your Savior, Lord, and Master and begin to follow Him and His commands, your words are also powerful.

Words like "I forgive you" change your condition in God's dimension. When forgiveness comes, a person is clean from sin in the unseen. This implies that before forgiveness came a person is dirty in the unseen realm.

Words like "Demon, I bind you in Jesus's name." That demon is immediately completely incapacitated in his world. "I gag you, demon, in the mighty name of Jesus Christ" actually closes the mouth and cripples the voice of the evil entity in the unseen. See how this works? God is still powerful, God's Word is still powerful, the name of Jesus is still powerful, and commands from Christians who are about their Father's business are also full of His power. God is still the "I Am."

Lord, help me to choose carefully what words I say since they carry Your weight and power behind them. Help me to use Your words and make a positive difference in the world around me. In Jesus's name, amen.

Prayer Is a Surgical Tool

> Confess your sins to each other and *pray for each other so God can heal you. When a believing person prays, great things happen.* (James 5:16, NCV)

SEAL Team 6 has been in the news a lot these last few years with everything that's gone on internationally. Those guys know it's war. They prepare for it, and they get the job done. Are you aware of the spiritual war you're in right now? Those who are unaware are destined to lose.

I hope this book helps you to have a new attitude about prayer. I hope to convince you that when you pray in the seen, great things happen in the unseen. Prayer is a surgical way to cut to the heart of the problem. It can get the job done. It's a surgical strike tool of enormous proportions. You can pray in Texas and affect a missionary in China. You can pray and truly make a difference whether you're 8, or 88, or 108. You can even pray if you're deaf, blind, mute, and on your deathbed. I honestly believe that if you could see what was happening in the unseen when you pray in the seen, you would pray more often, more specifically, and more fervently.

Lord, forgive me for underestimating the atomic power of prayer. Help me to pray with a new attitude and a new level of faith and commitment. In Jesus's name, amen.

Pray for the Lost, Not Just Sick Christians

> When *you pray for things, you don't get them because you want them for the wrong reason*—for your own pleasure. (James 4:3, GWT)

I think we've missed the boat on prayer, and not just because we've had a lackadaisical attitude toward it, but because we use prayer as though God was our Santa Claus in the sky. Most churches have focused their prayer lists on sick Christians. You know what? If they die, they go to heaven! Let's focus our prayers on the ones who are going to die and go to hell. That's what God is focused on!

Put prayers for loved ones in your pocket, in your billfold, on the back of your closet doors, on the side of your refrigerators, on the dash of your cars, and every other place where you'll be reminded to repeat them. Keep them on your lips all the time.

Lord, help me to be focused on Your agenda when I pray. Forgive me for always being so selfish in my prayers in the past. Remind me to use prayer as an evangelistic way to plow the ground for Your gospel of peace and salvation. In Jesus's name, amen.

Bible Stories Have a Purpose

> Now *these things* which happened to our ancestors *are illustrations of the way* in which *God works,* and they were written down to be a warning to us who are the heirs of the ages which have gone before us. (1 Cor. 10:11, Phillips)

> *These things happened* to them *as examples for us.* They were written down to warn us who live at the end of the age. (1 Cor. 10:11, NLT)

> *The things that happened* to those people are examples. They were written down *to teach us,* because we live in a time when all these things of the past have reached their goal. (1 Cor. 10:11, NCV)

Bible stories have a specific purpose: they illustrate how God is at work around us, they are examples for us to learn to follow, and they are meant to teach us how to make a difference for the kingdom in the world around us.

Lord, help me to study Your Word and learn the things I need to from the stories You have shared there so I can make a difference in the world around me. In Jesus's name, amen.

God's People Marked the Land

> *The Lord* appeared to Abram and *said,* "*I will give this land to your* descendants." So Abram built an altar there *[Shechem]* to the Lord, who had appeared to him. (Gen. 12:7, NCV)

Notice the very first thing Abram did when God promised him the land. He built an altar. An altar to the true and living God was a unique marker on the land. Altars to the pagan gods were very different—they were made of cut stones and in a specific shape. So altars to Jehovah God were very different. In fact, Abraham, Isaac, and Jacob built altars in Shechem, Bethel, Mount Moriah, Hebron, and Beersheba. These actually surround the heart of the land of Israel.

There are examples of markers on the land throughout the Bible, and I'll mention some of them in this section, but for a more complete list, please refer to "Markers on the Land" in the appendix.

Land markers and symbols are reminders of God. Many Christians today wear a cross around their neck or put a bumper sticker on their vehicle. It's good to be reminded of your connection to God. Jews did this by wearing scriptures on their bodies and also placing them on their gates and doorposts. This was commanded in Deuteronomy 6.

Many Jews still put a mezuzah on their gates and doorposts. It's a small box attached to the doorframe of each outside door. The box contained Scriptures about God and His promises to protect His people. Jews touch it or kiss it when they leave their home and also when they return. It's a reminder of their connection to God and His promise to protect them. He protects them when they are in their home, and He protects their possessions when they are away from it. The biblical principle here is simple: gates and doorposts protect, and God's Word is a shield of protection. Covenant people have the covenant Maker on their side, defending their home.

Lord, everything I have is Yours. Thank You for letting me use it on a temporary basis. I now dedicate myself and all of my possessions to be used to Your glory however You see fit. In Jesus's name, amen.

Israel Disobeyed

> The people of *Israel* are like vines that used to pro-
> duce fruit. The more fruit they produced, the more
> altars they built. The more their land produced, the
> more *stone markers they set up to honor other gods.*
> (Hosea 10:1, GWT)

Israel did the opposite of what they were told to do.
They set up land markers to honor the demonic gods that
the Canaanites had worshiped. God is a jealous god and
wants us separate from the rebellious angels who followed
Satan in rebellion and became part of his evil, demonic
team. So He swore to get His revenge:

> They are hypocrites. Now they must take their pun-
> ishment. *God will tear down their altars and destroy
> their stone markers.* (Hosea 10:2, GWT)

Satan has forces in the United States of America
too. And in my opinion, he has put his best warriors in
Washington, DC, and in Hollywood, California; and this
has been a very effective strategy. He has taken the land. I
say we mark it off and take it back, one house, one business,
one church at a time in the mighty name of Jesus Christ.

Lord, I now realize that greed is idolatry (Col. 3:5). And anything I place above You in my life can also become an idol. Forgive me for being just as unfaithful as Israel. Help me from now on to be a willing servant who honors You with every thought and every deed and every word I speak every day of my life. In Jesus's name, amen.

God Marked His People

> All must be circumcised. Your bodies will bear the mark of my everlasting covenant. (Gen. 17:13, NLT)

Remember when David went to visit his brothers who were in Saul's army? When he arrived at the Israelite camp, he discovered that Goliath had taunted Israel for forty days and invited them to send out a champion to fight him? Do you remember what David said?

> "*Who is this uncircumcised Philistine*, that he should defy the armies of the living God?" (1 Sam. 17:26, NKJV)

What was David really saying? He was saying, "I am circumcised. I am in covenant with the true and living Jehovah God. Who does this guy who doesn't have a covenant with God think he is? I don't care if he's twenty feet tall! Give me my sling and five stones. I got this, because I've got God on my side."

David understood covenants. He also understood that all other lesser gods answer to the one true God. And he expected God to come through and make sure he won because he was in an eternal covenant with Him. He was right.

By the way, have you ever wondered why he wanted five stones instead of two or three or ten? Goliath had four brothers. He was so confident in God that he figured he only needed one stone per giant.

God has always worked by covenant. There are seven main covenants in the Bible:

1. In Eden giving man dominion over the earth (Gen. 1:28).
2. With Adam removing them from Eden (Gen. 3:23–24).
3. With Noah promising God would never flood the world again (Gen. 9:8–10).
4. With Abram promising him land and descendants (Gen. 17:9).
5. With Moses and Israel, giving them the law (Exod. 24:7).

6. With David, promising his descendant would rule eternally (2 Kings 8:19).
7. With Christians, involving the New Covenant, which Jesus sealed with His blood and mentioned as he took the Passover meal with the disciples right before He went to the cross at Calvary (Heb. 13:20).

Circumcision was the mark of the covenant, beginning with Abram and continuing on through the Mosaic and Davidic Covenants. God marked his people, and the mark was not optional.

In fact, there's an interesting reference to this, right after Moses met God at the burning bush and before he returned to Egypt to free Israel. Moses had apparently failed to circumcise one of his sons, and God was about to kill him. The Amplified Version of the Bible offers some interesting insights about this event:

> Along the way at a [resting-] place, *the Lord met [Moses] and sought to kill him* [made him acutely and almost fatally ill]. [Now apparently *he had failed to circumcise one of his sons*, his wife being opposed to it; but seeing his life in such danger] Zipporah took a flint knife and cut off the foreskin of her son and cast it to touch [Moses'] feet, and said, surely

a husband of blood you are to me! When He let [Moses] alone [to recover], Zipporah said, a husband of blood are you because of the circumcision. (Exod. 4:24–26, AMP)

God has marked His people from the time of Abram forward. Until Jesus came, only the males could have the mark. Since the women were the property of the men back then, women were part of the elect of God through their connection to their "marked" men. Jesus came and changed all that, establishing a new style of mark that could be placed on females too (baptism).

Lord, thank You for providing a way for Your people to always be in relationship with You. Thank You for caring, for protecting, for providing. Thank you that the promises You gave Abraham are available to us all through faith (Gal. 3:14). In Jesus's name, amen.

God Is Still Marking His People

In him *you were also circumcised*. It was not a circumcision performed by human hands. But it was a removal of the corrupt nature in the circumcision performed by Christ. This happened when you were placed in the tomb with Christ *through baptism*. (Col. 2:11–12, GWT)

Colossians reveals a covenant principle that is often overlooked: baptism is spiritual circumcision. Baptism places you symbolically in the tomb with Christ, circumcising you in an unseen way. It removes the corruption, and you rise from the waters of baptism to walk a new life. I don't act like the old "Steve" after baptism. People are supposed to notice the difference in my life, and I'm supposed to bring the aroma of Christ to the atmosphere wherever I go.

The principle here, I hope, is crystal clear: God has always marked his people. Under the Old Covenant, He chose circumcision, but technically that continues under the New Covenant, since baptism is spiritual circumcision. It's a mark of freedom and eternity, and it opens the door to the indwelling of the Holy Spirit of God Himself. What a privilege and honor available to everyone through this faith-mark of Christianity! Have you got your mark?

Lord, thank You for marking all Your people with a sign of redemption. Remind me that baptism without faith is just getting wet, and that baptism places an unseen mark on me that I now belong to You. Thank You for that mark. In Jesus's name, amen.

With these biblical thoughts as a backdrop, I'm about to share some bizarre stories with you. Understand that I'm uncomfortable sharing this—in lectures or in this document—because of my conservative Christian background.

But I testify here that it's the truth rather than an active imagination embellished with literary expertise. I'm not an expert anyway, and I wouldn't ever want to lead anyone astray from God's truth in His Holy Word.

So if you are as uncomfortable reading them, we're in the same boat. But the truth needs to be heard. And I pray it changes your prayer life and your awareness of the spiritual realm.

Finally, please be forewarned that some of the subsequent material is R-rated. By this I mean that it's scary, eye-opening, and even sinister in some ways to be peeking into this little known reality of battles between good and evil in the unseen. Pray that God will help you discern truth here and that He will enable you to apply it in your daily life in such a way as to help others find their way into the light of the kingdom and a daily peace and confidence in God's ability to guide you through your future life in His service.

Overview of Bill's Story

> God didn't set us up for an angry rejection but for salvation by our Master, Jesus Christ. He died for us, a death that triggered life. Whether we're awake with the living or asleep with the dead, we're alive with him! *So speak encouraging words to one another.*

Build up hope so you'll all be together in this, no one left out, no one left behind. I know you're already doing this; just keep on doing it. (1 Thess. 5:11, The Message)

I consider myself nondenominational; and I'm happy to speak, lecture, or offer a series of presentations to any kind of church anywhere. But I do have a regular place of attendance not far from my house.

One of the leaders in the local church I attend when I'm not speaking somewhere else called one day. "I have a friend who's very upset. Would you be willing to talk to him?"

"What's wrong?" I asked innocently.

"He says he has demons on his property. Can you help?"

"Probably not," I replied. "But I can at least talk to him and pray with him."

So the meeting was arranged.

I met Bill, and he began to tell me his sad story. He really got my attention when he used the word *suicide*. He was literally considering suicide because of what he was experiencing. This woke me up to the seriousness of his situation. So I began to pray about how to respond. Bill is talking; I am praying.

A weird Old Testament verse popped into my mind, from Deuteronomy 6: "Put my word on your gates and doorposts."

How does that help? I thought. But then it clicked, and I knew what to say.

"Bill, don't kill yourself. The Bible is full of bizarre stories, right? Talking snakes, walking on water, a virgin birth, and resurrections. Also, God is so powerful that He simply spoke the world into existence, right? And His word is still powerful. He's the great 'I Am,' not the great 'I Used to Could,' right?"

"Right," Bill responded.

"Okay," I continued, "let's try something crazy and bizarre. Let's put Bible verse stakes on the corners of your property and see what God does."

With a very serious look on his face, Bill said, "Okay. At this point, I'll try anything."

Once we did this, Bill's whole life changed. He became a Christian the next week.

(More details of this whole story can be read in the appendix section called "The Original Stake Story," but for brevity's sake, I put this quick overview here so you can see the sequence that led to a firestorm of stake placements and fantastic stories that you can read on and experience.

Lord, please give me the words of encouragement I need at the very moment I need them most. Give me the wisdom to say them with the right tone and order. Grant me the boldness to speak up when necessary. And open the heart of the other person so they can receive them before it's too late for them. In Jesus's name, amen.

Bible-Based Thoughts Based on This Event:

Demons work to instill fear in the heart of their target.
Demons promote discouragement that might lead to suicide.
Demons can be stationed in a specific territory (like Bill's property).
Demons can be expelled through prayer and the posting of scriptures.

Selling Bill's House

The Lord will curse the evil person's house, but he will bless the home of those who do right. (Prov. 3:33, NCV)

Bill ended up going through a bankruptcy. I knew he had put his house up for sell to help pay some of his debt. He had gotten a job about two hours away and was living in a travel trailer. About six months after we staked out his place, I called him to see how he was doing.

"Everything is great," he told me. "I'm working hard and doing good. I pray for you every day, Steve."

"Thanks, Bill," I replied. "I can feel your prayers. I was wondering if you ever sold your house."

"Funny you should call. I finally sold it. It was on the market for four years. It was a nice home in a nice area, but in four years we never had an offer. In fact, we never had anyone even look at the place. I got to thinking about that, and I thought, 'Steve taught me what to do and how to pray over land.' So I followed your example, and we sold it for cash in just two weeks."

Let me tell you something, reader: only God can do that.

Lord, thank you for saving Bill and revealing Your power in his life. Thank You for Bill's example and act of faith. May his example help many others. In Jesus's name, amen.

Bible-Based Thoughts Based on This Event:

Demons sometimes might be able to prevent property from being sold.

Rental House

Paul stayed two full years in his own rented house and welcomed all people who came to visit him. (Acts 28:30, NCV)

Two of my good friends in the men's group at my church share some rental properties. One of their renters was an elderly woman who had been in the home for many years.

After she passed away, they did some updating to enhance the value for potential renters.

It didn't rent.

They did more updating. Spending quite a bit of money. It still didn't rent.

In fact, it had been over six months, and there was no hope in sight. So they decided to put stakes with Bible verses on the corners of the property to accompany their prayers (a simple act of faith—not a magic formula).

It rented just forty-eight hours later.

Only God can do that.

Lord, forgive me. Much of my life has been dedicated to my own kingdom instead of Yours. Thank You for revealing Yourself and Your power in this simple act of faith. I pray it becomes a witness to many others. In Jesus's name, amen.

Bible-Based Thoughts Based on This Event:

Demons sometimes might be able to keep rental property from renting.

Demonic Nightmares

When *an evil spirit leaves* a person, it goes into the desert, seeking rest but finding none. (Matt. 12:43, NLT)

Honestly, because of my very conservative Christian background, I went home and thought, *How am I going to write this story and not look weird to all of my friends?*

I got a call one day from a teacher. "Is it true," she began, "that your next book is about demons and prayer and spiritual warfare?"

'Yes," I replied. "Why?"

"Then I've got to come talk to you right now," she continued. "Can I come over?"

"Sure. Come on over."

When she arrived, you could almost see the fear in her bloodshot eyes. We sat in the living room, and her story came spilling out.

She had been on a mission trip with her church to a foreign country. After she returned, she had demonic nightmares. This had never occurred before in her life. They were very real, extremely frightening, and gave her the feeling of being violated in every possible way. She woke up in terrified a cold sweat and remembered every awful detail. Then she was too frightened to go back to sleep. In the low light in her room when she awoke, she could see figures in the darkness—not clearly—but absolutely present and demonic. She couldn't feel safe in her home anymore and was exhausted from the lack of sleep. "What should I do?" she demanded.

Much later, I discovered that Job 4:13–17 revealed a demonic encounter that was exactly what she had described:

> It came to me in a disturbing vision at night, when people are in a deep sleep. Fear gripped me, and my bones trembled. A spirit swept past my face, and my hair stood on end. The spirit stopped, but I couldn't see its shape. There was a form before my eyes. In the silence I heard a voice say, "Can a mortal be innocent before God? Can anyone be pure before the Creator?" (Job 4:13–17, NLT)

Keep in mind that Satan is called the accuser:

> The *accuser* of our brothers and sisters, who accused them day and night before our God, has been thrown down. (Rev. 12:10)

So here we have an "accusing" by a demonic entity.

I really didn't know what to suggest, but could feel her desperation; and my mind raced through everything I knew, looking for some tidbit that might help. Without really thinking, I asked, "Did you bring anything back with you?"

She thought for a moment and then answered, "Two things. A brochure about one of the local gods worshipped there and a letter from a lady I studied the Bible with."

"What did the letter say?" I inquired.

She hesitated, then answered, "Well," she began, "it said, 'Thanks for coming, but Buddha is the true God. Your God is not the true God."

"Okay," I replied, "I have two suggestions for you if you're willing."

"I'll do anything," she answered. "At this point, I'm scared to go to sleep."

"First," I began, "burn the brochure about the local god. And burn the letter from the woman."

"Second," I continued, "stake out your place." Since she lived in an apartment and didn't own the property, I encouraged her to stand the stakes in the four most remote corners. She complied. Then she prayed for God to make her home a place of peace, privacy, and safety from all evil in the name of Jesus Christ.

The nightly episodes of terror abruptly stopped. Problem solved by the Word of God.

Lord, thank You for the power of Your word and your promises. Thank You for protecting and providing. Please make my home a place of peace and safety just like You did for her. In Jesus's name, amen.

Bible-Based Thoughts Based on This Event:

Demons can act today just as they did in ancient times.

Demons may attach themselves to literature on demonic gods.

Demons can be persistent, returning to the same place night after night.

Demons may attach to seemingly innocent items that can be given to you.

God's Word can protect you from continual nocturnal demonic harassment.

Demonic Nightmares Returned

When *an evil spirit comes out of a person*, it travels through dry places, looking for a place to rest, but it doesn't find it. So *the spirit says, "I will go back to the house I left."* (Matt. 12:43–44, NCV)

The most comfortable place for a demonic spirit, I have learned, is the place where it's already been. A familiar spirit desires greatly to go back where it has been—which also coincides with the fact that bad habits are hard to break. There's a definite connection between the human tendency to relapse and the spiritual being to revisit familiar territory and continue to entice you to experience and enjoy evil.

The lady I just described who had experienced her terrifying nightmares coming to an end called me back one day.

"The nightmares are back," she began in a panic. "What did I do wrong?"

"Tell me about them," I inquired. She did, and it was much the same as before. Same verbiage. Same fear. Same panic. The exact same desperation was in her voice. She had lay in her bed with every light on, trembling with panic, waiting for morning to dawn so she could call me and ask what to do.

My first thought found voice: "Did you have any visitors in your home yesterday?" I asked.

There was a moment of silence—like it hadn't dawned on her that another human could bring a demon into her personal, protected territory.

"Yes," she said very softly, as if the event was replaying in her mind like a familiar movie. "Just one," she concluded.

When she didn't continue with any details, I asked gently, "Who was it?"

"A man I've been seeing." She spoke this softly too, as if she really knew deep down that this man might not be of the highest character. But lonely people don't always use wisdom as they search for a companion, do they?

Not wanting to get too personal but sensing that this individual was the root of her new problem, I gently asked, "Was there any physical contact?"

"Yes."

"That's the problem," I responded. "You invited evil in by inviting a person who is personally involved in evil. And your physical contact with him—however innocent it might have been—also invited the unseen evil on him right into your place of safety. And it's not safe right now."

"What do I do?"

"Sever contact with the man," I suggested, "and clean up the house again, just like you did before. Ask God to forgive you and to give you discernment for this in the future."

All this she did. Plus she added an additional set of stakes, a prayer sticker on her car, and prayers stickers on every window and door.

Early the next morning, I texted her, "How did you sleep?"

"Great," she quickly replied. "It worked." Then she thanked me. Then I thanked God, the Great Protector.

Lord, sometimes I return to the evil thing I thought I had learned to avoid. Forgive me—again. Cleanse me from the inside out—again. And help me to do better in the future. Fill me with Your Spirit and lead me closer to You each day. I don't want anything in my life to separate me from You. In Jesus's name, amen.

Bible-Based Thoughts Based on This Event:

Demons sometimes go right back to where they just came from.

Demons that have been expelled for a time are still near, hoping to return.

Demons can attach themselves to people who are actively participating in evil.

Demons attached to evil people who penetrate and invade the defenses

of a protected person can then remain inside those defenses.

Demons can be expelled a second time (after reinvasion).

Staking Out a Public School

Then he said, "I tell you the truth, unless you *turn from your sins and become like little children*, you will never get into the Kingdom of Heaven." (Matt. 18:3, NLT)

The teacher who was having demonic nightmares was so excited about how the stakes worked for her that she couldn't wait to tell the principal at her school—especially since they were best friends. After explaining the whole story to her, the principal responded with, "Do you think Steve would be willing to come stake out our school?"

"I don't know," the teacher responded. "I'll ask him."

She called me that night and explained the situation. The campus was in turmoil, and most of it was centered around one male teacher. There were problems among the students, among the teachers, among the staff, and even with the parents. All told, it had become an awful place to work because of the difficulties this man was causing on many different levels.

She called me to explain all this and then popped the question, "Would you be willing to come stake out our school?" I agreed on one condition: we had to do it at night when no one was there to see us do it. After all—it was public property; we didn't want to get into trouble...

So one evening on a cool winter night we did the deed. We had a flashlight, four stakes, a sledgehammer, and a key to the front gate. We prayed together at each corner after reading the verses and placing the protective corner marker. We prayed for the children who attended there, the teachers who taught there, the administrators who oversaw the curriculum and programs there, and the parents of the kids. After the last stake was in place and the prayer was finished, I turned to the principal and teacher and said, "You know, there's going to be some angry demons tomorrow morning when they can't get in here anymore. We just put an impenetrable wall around this school."

They looked at me and sort of giggled. "You might be right," they responded with a smile. I really don't know why I said that—it just felt like the thing to say at the time.

> All of *God's* words have proven to be true. He *is a shield to those who come to him for protection.* (Prov. 30:5, GWT)

I didn't hear from either one of these ladies for about nine months. It was right after *My Search for Prayers Satan Hates* hit Amazon. The teacher called and asked my wife about going out to eat with us.

As we sat together at a local café, I asked offhandedly, "By the way, how is everything at the school now—since we staked it out?"

"Wonderful," she quickly replied. "All the problems are gone, and it's now a great place to work. There is peace there, and we're all great friends focused on a common goal: helping the kids."

"Really? That's great," I responded. "So what happened to the man who was the main cause of all the problems?"

"He died," she said.

"Wait a minute, what?" I asked. "Was he old?"

"No, he was a young man."

No one knew anything about the stakes except the three of us.

I don't really understand it all. But I can tell you for sure that God's Word is still powerful. He's not the great "I Used to Could." He's still the great "I Am." And prayer still works. Praise His Holy Name.

Lord, thank You for helping this campus and delivering it and all these children from the evil beings that had been attacking them. Bless those children to do great things for You and Your kingdom. In Jesus's name, amen.

Bible Based Thoughts Based on This Event:

Demons can target schools and very young children.

God's Word is still powerful enough to protect your children.

God's power can still kill humans who are allied with His enemies.

It's All about Faith

Faith is the confidence that what we hope for will actually happen; it gives us assurance about things we cannot see. (Heb. 11:1, NLT)

These stories and the "Kingdom Stakes" as they have come to be called have literally changed my life. As one story led to another, one invitation to speak led to another in another state, and on and on it has gone. "Stake Stories," as they are often called, have led me to be known as "The Stake Guy." Strange, but true.

Occasionally, people with a strong, faithful prayer life have been casually offended at the idea of placing stakes with Bible verses on them and the possibility that they make a greater difference than prayer alone can make. I understand this sentiment completely. I began this journey reluctantly, doubting I heard from God correctly and puzzled at the brazen idea that it did actually work. But real-life examples, one after another, kept presenting themselves, and I've been forced to travel this path. God has dragged me "kicking and screaming," so to speak.

This led me back to the Bible, searching for biblical precedence. And I was shocked to find it in many different examples. I have chosen here to just share a few, and I invite you to pray, study God's Word, and think on these things.

Jericho.

Consider the story of the children of Israel conquering Jericho.

While the Canaanites (including the people of the border city of Jericho) were capable and experienced warriors, the Israelites were untrained and untested. Not only had their parents and ancestors just spent 430 in slavery in Egypt, they themselves had just spent the last forty years in the desert simply gathering manna and following God's pillars of cloud by day and fire by night. It's not like they had been in training with capable teachers during their journey.

So they crossed the Jordan at flood stage:

> When the priests who were carrying the chest came to the Jordan, their feet touched the edge of the water. *The Jordan had overflowed its banks completely*, the way it does during the entire harvest season. But at that moment the water of the Jordan coming downstream stood still. It rose up as a single heap very far off, just below Adam, which is the city next to Zarethan. The water going down to the desert sea (that is, the Dead Sea) was cut off completely. *The people crossed opposite Jericho.* (Josh. 3:15–16, CEB)

Then they camped out near Jericho. Per God's specific instructions, they marched around the city in silence for seven days. Then on the seventh day, they marched around the city seven times and blew the shofar, and the mighty fortress walls fell outward (I have read that this still baffles archeologists today). Then Israel rushed in and killed all the inhabitants except Rahab and her family. She lived high on the wall, which is how the Jewish spies escaped the Jericho authorities:

> Then, since *Rahab's house was built into the town wall*, she let them down by a rope through the window. (Josh. 2:15, NLT)

Her home in the wall had remained intact:

> Meanwhile, Joshua said to the two spies, "Keep your promise. *Go to the prostitute's house and bring her out, along with all her family*." (Josh. 6:22, NLT)

Could God have brought the walls down without a seven-day waiting period? Yes.

Could God have brought the walls down without the marching? Yes.

Could God have brought the walls down without trumpets? Yes.

But *marching around Jericho was an act of faith—a demonstration of faith*—that helped to make the walls come down.

Lord, thank You for the example of Jericho and for the reminder that, even though You are the One making things happen, I am involved and connected to it through my actions. In Jesus's name, amen.

Baptism

> Anyone who believes and is baptized will be saved.
> (Mark 16:16, NLT)

Baptism without faith is just getting you wet. That's all. Baptism without faith doesn't connect you to Jesus or God in any way. Baptism without faith doesn't get you clean—you don't even use soap.

But baptism with faith is special, unique, life changing (even your eternal life). It connects you to God (Col. 3:3), it's somehow connected to salvation (1 Pet. 3:21), it connects you to Jesus (Rom. 6:2–4) and resurrection (Rom. 6:8). It's included in the great commission (Matt. 28:18–20), it's spiritual circumcision (Col. 2:11–12), and it's the beginning of a new life (2 Cor. 5:17). It ushers in the Holy Spirit (Acts 2:38), and it's not something that Christians should delay in doing (Acts 22:16). God could have acknowledged Jesus as His Son anytime during His life—from His birth in Bethlehem to His death on Calvary—but He did it at His baptism (Matt. 3:16–17).

Actually there are at least twenty-four things that happen at baptism, but none of that applies if it's not done as an act of faith that Jesus Christ is the Messiah, the Son of the living God.

It's a symbol ordained by God, not man (John 1:33). Baptism demonstrates your intent to change your life and live for God (Rom. 6:4), and it's an appeal to Him for forgiveness (Matt. 3:6). It's a visible sign of your faith in Jesus as Savior, Lord, and Master.

Sure, God can save people without baptism if He wants, but since it's commanded (Acts 10:48) and since Jesus did it as an example for us (Mark 1:9), wouldn't you agree that it's rebellious and even sinful to refuse it? I've yet to find someone who claims to be a Christian who says it's okay to refuse baptism because that would be disobedient.

Bottom line: *baptism is an act of faith—a demonstration of faith*—that is part of your connection to God and the eternal realm. And it makes everything else work and make sense because it's a visible, public response to God's offer of eternal life with Him.

Lord, thank You for baptism. Thank You for all the connections baptism brings with it. Thank You especially for how it connects us to You. Forgive me for downplaying it in the past. I know Satan hates baptism because it bears witness that we are committing publicly to a life centered on kingdom purposes from that moment on. In Jesus's name, amen.

Prayer

> Admit your sins to each other, and *pray for each other*
> *so that you will be healed.*

> *Prayers offered by those who have God's approval are*
> *effective.* (James 5:16, GWT)

If you asked twenty people what prayer is, you'd probably get twenty answers. It's an act of worship, since you're asking a superior Being for help with a current problem. It's an expression of need to One who you feel is capable of rendering the aid you request. It's a connection to God the Creator.

Prayer changes the future. If you don't believe that, don't bother praying.

Prayer at its core is an admission of an unseen realm, where unseen beings are fighting over you and where you'll spend eternity.

I've often said that if we could see what's happening in the unseen when we pray in the seen, we'd pray more often, more specifically, and more fervently.

> "I will give you the keys of the kingdom of heaven,
> *and whatever you bind on earth shall be bound in*

heaven, and whatever you loose on earth shall be loosed in heaven." (Matt. 16:19, ESV)

You can pray if you're 8 or 88 or 108. You can pray if you're deaf, blind, and mute. You can pray in Texas and change something in Brazil. You can pray to help someone when you're on your deathbed. Prayer is powerful—very powerful. Never ever forget that.

But one thing prayer is that's usually overlooked is that *prayer is an act of faith—a demonstration of faith—*that makes a difference in our lives.

Lord, thank You for ordaining the avenue of prayer. Thank You for letting me be a part of what You choose to do here and now. Help me to choose my words wisely, and remind me to put Your agenda above my own. In Jesus's name, amen.

The Lord's Supper

> He took a cup of wine and gave thanks to God for it. He gave it to them and said, "Each of you drink from it, for this is *my blood*, which *confirms the covenant between God and his people.* It is poured out as a sacrifice to forgive the sins of many." (Matt. 26:27–28, NLT)

The Lord's Supper is a symbol of fellowship between God and Christians—His covenant people. It connects us to God. It's a reminder of resurrection, which is meant to encourage us as we grow old and feeble and see all our friends and relatives die. It represents the body and blood of Jesus Christ, our Savior. It's a ritual that helps us remember that He did for us so we could live with Him. Again, again, it's an admission of the unseen realm.

*Taking the Lord's Supper is an act of faith—a demonstration of faith—*that requires our participation: mind, body, and spirit.

Lord, thank You for establishing a reminder of our connection to You through Your Son Jesus. Help me never to neglect this or take it for granted. In Jesus's name, amen.

Satan's Links to the Physical World

> You used to live in sin, just like the rest of the world, obeying *the devil—the commander of the powers in the unseen world.* He is the spirit *at work in* the hearts of *those who refuse to obey God.* (Ephes. 2:2, NLT)

Satan has a variety of links and lures in our physical world designed to lead us away from God and trap us. Some of the things on this will surprise you, but remember: God is the ultimate, complete, and final authority in the whole universe. Any talisman, good luck charm, or "crystal ball" to help know future happiness or freedom from fear that's not mentioned in Scripture is not from God, and therefore from Satan.

Tarot cards are supposed to tell you about your future. They are evil. God knows your future, and you should only consult Him on it:

> You know what I am going to say even before I say it, Lord. (Ps. 139:4, NLT)

Palm reading is also supposed to reveal how long you will live. God knew that before you were even born:

> You saw me before I was born. Every day of my life was recorded in your book. Every moment was laid out before a single day had passed. (Ps. 139:16, NLT)

A rabbit's foot is carried to bring good luck. God determines who will succeed and who will fail:

> We may throw the dice, but the Lord determines how they fall. (Prov. 16:33, NLT)

Dream catchers are promised to "filter out" bad dreams in the night. Satan is the god of this world (2 Cor. 4:4), and he rules a kingdom of darkness (Col. 1:13). Only God can protect you in the night:

> *He will protect his faithful ones*, but the wicked will disappear *in darkness*. No one will succeed by strength alone. (1 Sam. 2:9, NLT)

Horoscopes are based on your birth date—your connection to the stars in the sky—and are supposed to warn you in advance so you can avoid problems. God's Holy Word is designed specifically for that purpose:

> *All Scripture is inspired by God* and is *useful* to teach us what is true and to make us realize what is wrong in our lives. It corrects us when we are wrong and teaches us to do what is right. (2 Tim. 3:16, NLT)

Crystals and some special jewelry offer hope against "negative energy." Pornography is the biggest industry in the world from the standpoint of total money spent. It promises sexual satisfaction in a variety of ungodly ways. But God designed marriage as the place to fulfill those desires:

> *Give honor to marriage, and remain faithful* to one another *in marriage. God will surely judge people who are immoral and those who commit adultery.* (Heb. 13:4, NLT)

Ouija boards promise answers about the future from an unseen spirit, but that spirit is a demon.

> One day as we were going down to the place of prayer, we met *a slave girl* who *had a spirit that enabled her to tell the future.* She earned a lot of money for her masters by telling fortunes. She followed Paul and the rest of us, shouting, "These men are servants of the Most High God, and they have come to tell you how to be saved." This went on day after day until *Paul* got so exasperated that he turned *and said to the demon within her, "I command you in the name of Jesus Christ to come out of her." And instantly it left her.* (Acts 16:16–18, NLT)

Pentagrams are a satanic symbol that more and more people are beginning to boldly display on everything from Web sites to statues to yard flags. Séance's and mediums promise to contact the dead, but God said to never consult them:

> "*Do not defile yourselves by turning to mediums or to those who consult the spirits of the dead.* I am the Lord your God." (Lev. 19:31, NLT)

Again, seeking anything other than God is idolatry, evil, and double-minded. It's like being baptized and holding one hand out of the water. That won't fly with God. It's all or nothing with Him.

Lord, You and You alone are my God, my Lord, my King, and my Master. I reject all other false gods in favor or You and Your power. I serve You, I live for You, and I pledge to follow Your commands. Use me to Your glory. Come soon and find me faithful. Then give me a place to live close to You. In Jesus's name, amen.

God's Links to the Physical World

> All honor and glory to *God* forever and ever! He is *the eternal King, the unseen one who never dies*, he alone is God. Amen. (1 Tim. 1:17, NLT)

The Bible is full of symbols that represent literal realities. These "God-Links" help us feel a connection to our Creator, and encourage us in our daily choices to remember that we are ambassadors of the King of kings.

The cross reminds us of Jesus, His sacrifice, His love, His suffering, and our adoption into the royal family because He took our place and got what we deserved. Communion is a visible, tangible reminder of our covenant with God. Baptism is a reminder of our personal commitment to follow Christ. The Bible is also a symbol. One Scripture reveals this in a unique way:

> And *there are also many other things which Jesus did. If they should be all recorded one by one [in detail]*, I suppose that even *the world itself could not contain (have room for) the books that would be written.* (John 21:25, AMP)

So you see, the Bible is a sampling of what Jesus did and a symbol of what you can do. You are a Bible story that will be told and retold in heaven. Keep that in mind as you make daily choices.

While Satan's links and lures try to get you to choose rebellion against God, God's links and lures encourage you to remember His promises and that rewards are in the cards for you if you choose Jesus and remain faithful.

Satan promotes instant gratification while God promises deferred gratification. Choose the later. It will be worth it. Guaranteed. By God Himself.

Lord, thank you for the memorials and symbols that remind me on a regular basis of my eternal, nonseverable connection to You. In Jesus's name, amen.

Don't Tell Anyone

> He replied, "*You are permitted to understand the secrets of the Kingdom* of Heaven, but others are not." (Matt. 13:11, NLT)

My wife is probably even more conservative than I am. And she's even more skeptical than me. If a Tide commercial comes on television, for example, bragging about how white it makes your clothes, it wouldn't be unlikely to hear her say, "I bet it doesn't work that well. Nothing can get clothes that white." It's just how she is.

So when all these bizarre stories began to happen—and many more that are shared in the coming pages—I would tell her all about it. She would smile and nod and quickly say, "That's great, honey! *Don't* tell anybody."

But the stories kept coming and kept coming, and they were often from very credible people. So her whole attitude has changed. I travel often now on speaking trips, and we usually talk on the phone every day. And she says, "What happened today?"

Again, God is not the great "I Used to Could." He's the great, "I Am."

Lord, open our eyes to how You are at work all around us. Then give us a willing heart to join Your work in however You see fit. In Jesus's name, amen.

Sticky Note Verses

> *These tablets were God's* work; the *words* on them were *written by God himself.* (Exod. 32:16, NLT)

I will remember their sins and their lawless deeds *no more.* (Heb. 10:17, ESV)

One day I got a phone call out of the blue from a lady who used to go to church with us. She and her family had moved to a city about an hour away because of her husband's job transfer.

"Steve," she began, "something made me call you today."

"Great to hear from you, Sue!" I replied. "What's going on?"

"Something strange," came the response. "We bought a new house, and we've been in it for a couple of months. When I'm here alone, I've noticed something weird.

When I was in high school—before I became a Christian—I sowed some wild oats. I did some drinking and ran with the wrong crowd. Lately, when I'm here at the house by myself, I begin to feel extremely guilty about all that. What could cause that?"

"Well," I began in response, "when you became a Christian, did God forgive you of all that?"

"Yes," she responded quickly.

"And does He remember your sins?"

At this, she paused for moment, as if turning the words over in her mind. Then she replied confidently, "No. The Bible says that He remembers our sins no more. In fact, He puts them as far away from us as the east is from the west."

"Very good. So if you are being reminded of your past sins, it's definitely not God. Who could it be?"

She was quiet for a moment. Then she said, "Satan or one of his demons."

> The *accuser of our brothers and sisters* has been thrown down to earth—the one who *accuses them before our God day and night.* (Rev. 12:10b, NLT)

"Right again."

"So what should I do?"

At this point, I told her about the stakes with Bible verses on them and all the wonderful results from real people with real problems.

We hung up after deciding she would try posting sticky notes all around her house—in every single room—with Bible verses on them.

It worked. She texted me an update two hours later. "All the guilt is gone. You're right, Steve. God's word is powerful."

Lord, thank You for Your everlasting promises that make a difference in our daily lives. Thank You for putting our sins far away from us and even forgetting them when we repent, turn to Jesus, and obey Your commands. In Jesus's name, amen.

Bible-Based Thoughts Based on This Event:

Demons definitely want you to feel guilty for all your past sins.

Demons want your guilty feelings to paralyze you from kingdom work.

Demons want to steal your joy if they can't steal your salvation (and they can't).

Remnants of an Idol

So Jacob told everyone in his household, "*Get rid of all your pagan idols*, purify yourselves, and put on clean clothing." (Gen. 35:2, NLT)

It was Saturday, it was cold, and the weather was threatening ice accumulations in the small town where I'd just arrived to give a four-day lecture series on demons, prayer, and spiritual warfare. The local church that had invited me had put an advertisement in the paper, calling the series "Demons vs. Prayer."

This was the first time I would give a series from my book *My Search for Prayers Satan Hates*, and I was anxious with excitement. I had lots of new slides for my PowerPoint presentation and was giddy with enthusiasm to share them.

But it didn't look like the weather was going to cooperate. An ice storm would ruin the attendance—not to mention the enthusiasm. When you have an auditorium only half full on Sunday morning you can't help but be a little deflated.

We prayed together about the weather and put it in the Lord's hands. I was at peace with whatever happened—big crowd or a precious few.

But then the conversation changed. I was staying with the minister and his family for the next few days of the meeting, and an alarming chain of events had just happened before I arrived. Their son had informed them he was gay. He was dropping out of college and pursuing an alternate lifestyle. He wasn't even coming home for Christmas. They were devastated.

The preacher had heard my story of the stakes and had gone so far as to go make some and place around his home—while the son still lived there. There had definitely been improvement in the boy's attitude and demeanor, but now they were at a loss. "What did we do wrong?" they implored. "Why didn't the stakes work?"

After all I had seen the stakes (as symbols of faith) accomplish, I too was at a loss.

"Well," I began thoughtfully, "I have seen situations in the past where there was something in the home that had been staked out that honored a foreign god. Things like demonic artwork, hidden drugs, pornography, or even a seemingly innocent item like a souvenir from a foreign country that turned out to honor an evil spirit."

The preacher's face went white. "Oh my goodness," he stated flatly.

"What is it?"

"A few years ago," he began, "when my boy was in high school, he went with me on a mission trip. It was a group of about twenty folks. We spent some time in a village in the bush and ended up converting and baptizing the entire population. It was an exciting time. At the end of our time there, the village chief allowed me to be the one who broke their small stone idol that sat in the center of the town. I raised it up over my head and threw it down hard on a rocky area. It cracked into many pieces. Then my son walked over and picked up some of the small stones, putting them in his pocket to take home."

He stood and rushed back to the boy's bedroom—the one I was about to stay in for the next five nights—and frantically searched it. But he didn't have to look far. There were some small rock fragments right there on the dresser. He stared at them in disbelief. "How could I have over-looked something so important?" he asked out loud. He grabbed them up and headed out the door to throw them far into the woods.

When he got back, we continued to search the room for ungodly objects. There was a stack of satanic artwork under the bed that the boy had drawn. Dragons with blood dripping from their teeth were among the many pages of art. He took them outside and burned them right away. He had never seen them before.

> *This great dragon*—the ancient serpent called *the devil, or Satan*, the one deceiving the whole world—was thrown down to the earth with all his angels. (Rev. 12:9, NLT)

Lord, I pray right now for whoever is reading this and thinking about their own home. Please bring to mind anything they have that honors a foreign god. And give them the courage to remove and destroy it—no matter how much they paid for it. In Jesus's name, amen.

Sleeping Near the Enemy

> *The Lord will be our* Mighty One. He will be like a wide river of *protection* that no enemy can cross, that no enemy ship can sail upon. (Isa. 33:21, NLT)

Here I was about to spend the next five nights in a room full of this boy's stuff. The drawers and closet were packed with his things, and there wasn't time to empty it all out right now—it was already 10:00 p.m. at night, and I was sleepy.

I had been on the road all day to get there, the weather was freezing, a coat of ice was expected to ruin church attendance for my presentations the next day, and I was exhausted. On top of all that, I had arrived at the preacher's home to find them distraught over the ungodly decisions their son was making. I had tried my best to encourage and comfort them. But now I had to sleep in that boy's bedroom, where we had just found demonic drawings and rock chunks from a village idol in Africa. Add to that, the black swords, breastplate, and helmet that hung on the walls in the room, and I felt like it was a recipe for disaster. What else was hidden in the overstuffed closet that was evil?

I have been in motel rooms and couldn't sleep. Many times those rooms were centers for pornography and prostitution. Sometimes I could just feel the evil present—left behind by former tenants. I needed a good night's rest to be ready for tomorrow—in case the weather cooperated and people actually showed up at church.

So I hit my knees in prayer beside the bed. "Lord," I prayed, "I'm really nervous about sleeping in the boy's room tonight. I don't know what else might be in here that dishonors You or honors a false god, and I need a *good night's rest* so I can do a good job telling others about you tomorrow. So I am asking for extra angelic protection while I'm here. In Jesus's name, amen."

I crawled under the covers and closed my eyes. I had left the closet light on so I could see to get up in the night if I needed to. I relaxed, knowing I had put it all in God's capable hands. But before I was sound asleep, it happened.

It happened at just that moment when you're dozing off into full sleep—but aren't quite there yet. I was laying flat on my back, breathing slowly, muscles relaxed, and my brain was shutting down. But I suddenly felt something press down on both my legs, right below the knees.

Who is in my room? I thought. *Is it someone sleepwalking or a burglar?* My mind rushed back toward consciousness, but I didn't want to jerk or rise up in a panic for fear that whoever was there had a knife or gun. I quickly raced through my options for response, not wanting to bring their reflexes down on me somehow. I decided to slowly open my eyelids and lift my head ever so slightly so as not to alarm them or let them know I was awake. So that's exactly what I did.

The light coming from the cracks around the closet door gave enough light that I could see shadows and objects in an eerie black-and-white style. But nothing and no one was there—that you could see with the human eye. And as soon as I peeked, the pressure on my legs quickly increased and my legs pressed farther down into the mattress. Then, just as rapidly, it was completely gone.

Immediately, my mind heard these words: "You prayed, I'm here, rest easy."

> For he will order his angels to protect you wherever you go. (Ps. 91:11, NLT)

My "extra-angelic protection" had arrived and was letting me know. I slept like a baby. And by that I don't mean I woke up crying every hour; I mean I slept very peacefully.

I awoke early the next morning, completely refreshed and ready to go. I always wake up early when I get to speak somewhere and share God's power. The threatening ice storm had fizzled, and although it was cold and wet, there was a big crowd at the morning assembly (another prayer answered).

In addition, I knew I could relax for the duration of my stay in that home.

Lord, thank You for answering these prayers. Thank You for sending the needed protection at just the time. Your timing is perfect. Remind me that You are always there, ready to send help when I call. In Jesus's name, amen.

Bible-Based Thoughts Based on This Event:

Prayer can sometimes affect the weather to reach the lost.

Demons can attach to physical objects and can go to wherever it is.

Angels can be dispatched to help us when we pray to God.

Angels sometimes let their presence be known.

A Porn Addiction :Part 1

A beautiful woman who lacks discretion is like a gold ring in *a pig*'s snout. (Prov. 11:22, NLT)

Billy was addicted to pornography—you know, where beautiful women who lack discretion allow people to take pictures of their bodies. He had been for over twenty years. He hid his porn behind the bullets and shotgun shells inside his gun safe. That was the one place his wife never looked.

In addition, he had a spending problem. He was on disability, and his wife was a teacher. They had two beautiful daughters. Billy would get a credit card his wife knew nothing about and charge all sorts hunting gear and porn he didn't want her to know about. Eventually, a bill would come to the house, and she would see it before he did. She would get angry and kick him out of the bedroom. Billy would then pay off the card and cut it up.

But the process kept repeating itself. A new card, charges for things he wanted but couldn't afford, then getting found out.

When I met Billy at church the week I spoke there, he had been sleeping in the guest bedroom for quite a while. Since his girls were both away at college, it was easy for Billy and his wife to hide their problems from them.

I had been invited to give a series of lectures in Billy's church on my book *My Search for Prayers Satan Hates*. We called the series "Demons vs. Prayer." It was scheduled for Sunday morning Bible class and worship, Sunday evening, and then was to continue for the following three evenings, ending on Wednesday night.

On Sunday morning, I showed verse after verse where God's people put markers on the land. I began by pointing out that when Abram made a covenant with God, he built an altar. Altars to the true God were from uncut stones. This was unique and quite different from the altars built to all the pagan gods. The altar was a "marker" on the land, sort of announcing that God was protecting the property where His people dwelled. (This was detailed earlier in this book.)

On Sunday evening, I presented a long list of demons actually named in the Bible. I also pointed out that each and every demon listed in Scripture is over a very specific territory, literally a marked-out area of responsibility. Sometimes it was a city, other times it was a region or wider area, and some were even listed as being dedicated to specific nations. This discovery was quite a shock to me. In fact, I have yet to find a demonic entity named in the Bible without the additional information of what he (or in some cases *she*) was specifically in charge of.

The congregation listed attentively and politely. Although this is a very relevant and biblical topic, I have found that many Christians have never heard sermons on it. They have heard of Satan and know of demons in the Bible, but the thought that these evil things could still be around seems to unsettle some folks—in spite of the scriptural indication in Ephesians 6 and many other places that they are real and very present, intelligent, and organized in their attacks on us.

I met Billy after the evening service. I like hunting and noticed Billy's new Drake duck-hunting jacket. It stuck out to me because it was just like one we had gotten for Blake, my middle son, for Christmas. I told Billy I liked his coat, and he told me he enjoyed my lessons.

Early the next morning, I got a voice mail from him: "Steve, this is Billy. I met you yesterday, and you commented on my duck-hunting jacket. I think God sent you here to save my life, my marriage, and my soul. I didn't know demons were real, but your lesson yesterday taught me otherwise. I need you to meet me at the church and pray over me. I have a demon."

Wow. Shocking, to say the least. Nothing like this had ever happened to me before.

I was already on the way to the church building when I got the message. The preacher pulled up when I did. He had gotten the same message. We didn't have to wait long. Billy pulled up about five minutes later, and we all went inside to the minister's office and shut the door. Billy looked serious and focused.

I was nervous. I didn't want to mess this up, and I was about to do something I'd never done before. I knew it was important and had eternal consequences. I was going to pray for Billy, but I wasn't sure what to say. I knew the Holy Spirit would help me, and then the thought occurred to me that I might want to remember exactly what I said so I could see what happened and then improve on it in the future if I was ever asked to do this again, so I asked Billy if I could video it. He said I could, so I set the phone up, and we began…

Billy explained that he knew he had a demon after hearing the lessons the day before because for many years he had been completely unable to pray or read the Bible. "Every time I try to read a chapter or pray to God, my mind starts jumbling up all the words and I can't concentrate. Yesterday I realized it was a demon that caused that."

> *Satan, who is the god of this world, has blinded the minds* of those who don't believe. They are unable to see the glorious light of the Good News. *They don't understand this message* about the glory of Christ, who is the exact likeness of God. (2 Cor. 4:4, NLT)

Check the appendix in the back of this book for the whole story about why I asked this, but the first I asked Billy was, "Can you say, 'Jesus is Lord'?"

He said, "Yes. Jesus is Lord."

"Okay," I replied, "now we're ready to start. Are you ready to quit this life of pornography and evil?"

"Yes," he said simply, "I want to be a good Christian husband and father.

"Lord," I prayed as my hands were on Billy's shoulders, "Billy is ready to turn from lies and evil and porn to a life of godliness. He renounces everything in his life that doesn't honor You. And in the name of Jesus Christ, we bind all evil spirits that are attached to him. Lord, we don't want to just run them off from Billy to bother other people. We ask they be bound in chains and gagged to silence and put in the pit until judgment day—the place mentioned in Jude 6 that is a holding cell for some evil fallen angels (demons). In Jesus's name, amen."

You also know about the *angels who* didn't do their work and *left their proper places. God* chained them with everlasting chains and *is now keeping them in dark pits* until the great day of judgment. (Jude 1:6, CEV)

"How do you feel now?" I asked Billy.

"I feel great," was his quick reply. "Now I want three sets of those stakes of yours with the Bible verses on them."

I had to go review my lesson for that evening's service, so I excused myself and left. I got only two blocks from the church building when a very unusual thing happened. I heard a sound. Loud. Piercing. And it seemed to be coming from right above the roof of my Jeep. A squeal? A screech? Was it a piercing scream? Was it a plane falling from the sky? My head was on a swivel, looking in the rearview mirror, front, and side to side. I couldn't see anything. But it was ear-piercing. And immediately following this first sound came a second, right on its tail. I've never been to a launching of a rocket, and I've never stood beside a 747 engine as it was taking flight, but the sound I heard was exactly what I had always imagined that would be like. Then it faded swiftly into the distance, as if the rocket was ascending rapidly out of sight. Then it was gone. Complete silence surrounded me.

I pulled off the road in shock. What in this world—or out of this world—was that? Was it an airplane falling from the sky? No. Was it the sound of some sort of nearby factory exploding? These thoughts and many more crossed the synapses of my mind in a nanosecond.

I grabbed my cell phone and called the church. "Preacher, is there anything around here that makes loud noises like this?" I quickly described what I'd heard.

"No. Nothing," was his reply.

"Then the thing we just cast out of Billy," I said, "is really mad."

I learned later that Billy put one set of stakes around his house and a second set on the corners of the property. He put a nail in the doorframe of each of his four outside doors and hung the third set on those nails, just like the Jewish mezuzah.

A thankful text came from Billy in the middle of the afternoon: "Thank you so much, Steve," he said. "For the first time in years, I can pray. And I'm reading the Bible right now. I can understand every word."

His wife came up to me at church the next night, hugging me with tears in her eyes. "You saved our marriage," she sobbed.

"No," I replied. "God did. But I am honored to have been a small part of helping."

Lord, open my eyes to people all around me who are just like Billy, and show me how to help them. In Jesus's name, amen.

Bible-Based Thoughts Based on This Event:

Demons use pornography to gain a foothold into your life.

Demons work to keep people from reading God's Word regularly.

Demons can confuse your mind so you can't pray or read the Bible

Demons often work to keep people from having an active prayer life.

Demonic footholds can become strongholds that separate you from God.

Demon removal can restore your marriage, your Bible study, and your prayer life.

Demons work to destroy marriages.

Porn Addiction: Part 2

I discovered that *a seductive woman is a trap more bitter than death.* Her passion is a snare, and her soft hands are chains. Those who are pleasing to God will escape her, but sinners will be caught in her snare. (Eccles. 7:26, NLT)

A short time after meeting Billy and helping him rid his life of demons, I was speaking at a city about 150 miles away and told his story. I only used his first name and felt sure no one would know him. I was wrong.

It was Saturday morning at a men's retreat. When the day was done, an older gentleman (about seventy-five years old) approached me and said, "Steve, was Billy's last name Smith?" (Not Billy's real last name.)

"Yes," I replied in shock, worried I had done the unthinkable by sharing far too much about Billy with a man who obviously knew him. My mind was racing because I had confirmed his suspicion before thinking through it.

Tears filled the man's eyes and rolled gently down his cheeks. "I know him, and I've been praying for him for over twenty years."

My shock deepened. "You're kidding," was all I could think to say.

But he wasn't finished.

"Let me tell you what else," he continued. "I had the same problem. It filled my mind with filth and almost cost me my marriage. But I confessed it, got help, and my wife was patient with me as I gradually got control over it. Eventually it had no hold over me at all. Finally, one night at 3:00 a.m., I heard a piercing scream right above our bed that woke me in terror. And then I heard, "Good-bye."

That's when I interrupted him. "Your assigned demon gave up on you and left because you had completely overcome that temptation," I stated as a fact.

"That's exactly what happened," he replied through a steady flow of tears. "That's exactly what happened."

Lord, how many others are caught in this same trap? What can I do to help them? Give me wisdom in helping others deal with this sort of universal temptation. Give me the right words for each person that will truly help them overcome. In Jesus's name, amen.

Bible-Based Thoughts Based on This Event:

Demons have a right to be in your life when you're still involved in evil.

Demons eventually finally give up and leave when you have overcome evil.

Sometimes, prayers are enough; but posting God's Word can make a great difference.

Gramp's Little Princess

But *the love of the Lord* remains forever with those who fear him. His salvation *extends to the children's children.* (Ps. 103:17, NLT)

Her little girl loved her Gramp! Every time they went to Gramp's house, she would run to him, yelling, "Graaaaamp!" jumping in his lap, wanting to hug and kiss and then read a book. The child was in kindergarten now, but it had been this way from the time she could talk.

One day the mother took the girl with her by the car dealership to sign some papers. While she was at the salesman's desk doing all the paperwork, the little girl was nearby in a small play area for children. That must have been when it happened.

A man—the kind of man who would give any mother an uneasy feeling—came up to the little girl and bent down, whispering to her softly, smiling, a little too close. He gently reached over and gave the girl a little pat on the back.

Her mother watched the entire exchange, and although nothing inappropriate happened (nothing that could be seen with the human eye), the whole episode gave the mom a very unsettling feeling in the pit of her stomach. But then he was gone. Just as quickly as he had appeared. Then the mom and her little angel left for Gramp's house.

"There's Gramps!" the mother told her daughter. But the little girl was anything but excited to see him. She sulked back and hid behind the mom—something she'd never ever done before. It was a complete personality change, and there seemed to be no explanation for it at all.

"Maybe she's just going through a shy stage," Gramps suggested. "Let's just give her some time and space." They did.

But nothing changed. This new response became the norm, and as the weeks progressed, there was no change in the little girl. She seemed completely terrified of Gramps. Puzzling, to say the least.

Soon it was time for the mom's monthly prayer group to meet and pray for the schools, teachers, and children of their community. The fellowship and subsequent prayer time went well, but as the mom and little girl got ready to go, one of the elderly ladies noticed the little girl. "Is she okay?" she asked the mother.

"I think so," replied the mom. "But she has been acting strangely ever since we went by the car dealership and a strange man bent down and talked quietly to her."

"That's what I thought," said the stately woman. "She has a demon. Bring her over here so we can pray for her." A group of Christian woman laid hands on the little girl, praying for her restoration and protection and binding any evil entity connected to her, casting it out of her life for good.

Prayers finished. The mother and daughter left the group—and went by Gramp's house. "Gramps!" the little girl squealed as she ran and jumped in his lap to hug and kiss him and ask to read a book. It was a complete reversal of her personality—back to how it had always been. She recognized, loved, and longed for Gramps again, like she had always done.

What happened? I'm not sure. What did the man say to her? Maybe it was, "Can I leave a friend with you?" I don't know, but evil forces are always trying to work their way into our lives in any way possible.

Lord, please bless and protect the little, innocent children. Deliver them from the evil that's so abundant in this present world. And teach me how to pray for them effectively. In Jesus's name, amen.

Bible-Based Theory:

Demons can sometimes attach to innocent children.

Demons can be prayed out of innocent little children.

Demons might sometimes be transferred to others through touch.

While adults are responsible and able to make decisions that either separate them from God or draw them closer to Him, children are innocent, and can be tricked into allowing evil to draw near. Adults can choose to slander someone or view porn, which gives Satan and his forces a "foothold." Footholds can become strongholds, addictions. Scripture reveals that Satan asked the Lord for His permission to attack Job in the Old

Testament and to attack Peter and the apostles in the New Testament. Little children aren't responsible (yet) for making these sort of weighty decisions. So, perhaps, the demon had to ask her for permission for something. Maybe he leaned close and asked her, "Sweetie, I have a really nice friend I'd like to leave with you. Is that okay?" She nodded. Then he patted her on the back. Maybe the touch enabled the transfer of the demon to the little girl—with her permission. Though if this is the case, she probably didn't understand what she was agreeing to.

The Flying Stake

> You are saying *some rather strange things*, and we want to know what it's all about. (Acts 17:20, NLT)

Jay lives in North Texas. He had heard me speak at his church a couple of years ago. When he saw I had stakes for sale on my Web site with Bible verses on them to put around your home as a symbol of God's protection and authority, he ordered some.

The package arrived, and he anxiously went outside with his hammer to place at the corners of his home. Each stake was nine inches long. A regular hammer should work fine in the soft yard right around his house.

He placed one of them in the ground and began to drive it in. It was already halfway down into the ground when something strange happened.

It's common when you're driving an object into the ground and hit something for that object to pop up and out of the hole. When this occurs, you simply move to another spot and try again. But that's not what happened to Jay.

The hammer glanced off, and the stake came out of the hole, but instead of popping up a few inches, it went ten feet in the air. Physics laws had been violated, and Jay knew it.

"At the time," he explained on the phone, "it freaked me out, but I was focused on the task and determined to finish the job."

"If there was a root or rock or any other object in the way, it would have been impossible for this plastic stake to penetrate it and go on in, so I decided to put it back into the same hole and try that first. It went right in all the way down. No roots. No rocks. And no reason for it to fly ten feet in the air."

Something or someone unseen didn't want it in there.

Lord, grant me a focused determination to finish the task at hand. Remind me that the Spirit in me is greater than the spirits that are in the world around me. In Jesus's name, amen.

Bible-Based Thoughts Based on This Event:

Demons can make strange things happen in the physical realm.

Demons don't want you to post God's Word around your home in faith.

Streaks on the Walls

Then the *priest will go in and examine the mildew on the walls. If he finds greenish or reddish streaks and the contamination appears to go deeper than the wall's surface, the priest will* step outside the door and *put the house in quarantine for seven days.* (Lev. 14:37–38, NLT)

When God was bringing Israel into Canaan, the Israelites were told they would live in a land of milk and honey (Exod. 3:8). They were being given houses they didn't build, and they would be harvesting crops and fruits and vegetables they didn't plant (Deut. 6:10–11). But then (in Leviticus 14), there was strange talk about streaks or mold or mildew appearing on the walls of the houses. If that occurred, they were to call a priest and get an inspection.

This always confused me. Why would you need a priest? Why wouldn't you just need a carpenter or a construction supervisor? What did religion have to do with it?

After a little research, I found the answer, and it's quite interesting. It's connected to Satan and demons and idol worship.

The Canaanites were idolatrous people. They worshipped a variety of demonic gods through the land. In that day and time, there were no banks, no vaults in secure buildings for your valuables. And since they viewed dedication to idols as a way to be protected by supernatural beings, they put idols of gold, silver, copper, and bronze in the walls of their homes.

This served a dual purpose. Since it was hidden in the walls, they could retrieve them if needed to redeem their monetary value. But this was also a safeguard. If they were captured and taken away and they later escaped and returned, they could retrieve their valuables—like a secure bank account.

This helped me to understand why a priest was called instead of a construction worker. It was truly a spiritual issue, which required a priest. The infected section was removed and reinspected at a later date. If it occurred again, this process was repeated. Some homes, however, were so dedicated to the local demon gods that they were eventually turned into a pile of rubble and abandoned and destroyed.

Suppose a person has taken away the old stones and plaster and put in new stones and plaster. *If mildew again appears* in his house, *the priest must come back* and check the house again. *If the mildew has spread* in the house, it is a mildew that destroys things; the house is unclean. Then *the owner must tear down the house, remove all its stones, plaster, and wood, and take them to the unclean place outside the city.* (Lev. 14:43–45, NCV)

Lord, forgive me for placing such a high value in the things of this world—just like the Canaanites did. Help me to focus on what's really valuable: my relationship with You. In Jesus's name, amen.

Bible-Based Thoughts Based on This Event:

Demons can be connected to valuable objects of gold and silver.

Demons can ruin the property beyond human ability to restore it.

Demons can inhabit things in your home that have become idols to you.

The "Haunted" Dorm Room

> This is the message we heard from Jesus and now
> declare to you: God is light, and there is no dark-
> ness in him at all. So we are lying if we say we have
> fellowship with God but go on living in spiritual
> darkness; we are not practicing the truth. But if we
> are *living in the light*, as God is in the light, then
> we have fellowship with each other, and the blood
> of Jesus, his Son, cleanses us from all sin. (1 John
> 1:5–7, NLT)

I made a visit to a Christian college a little while after
the event with Bill and the stakes and shared it with a dorm
supervisor there.

"Awesome," he responded. "God is powerful! I really
believe this stuff. We had a similar situation here on campus one year in the dorm I was in charge of."

"What happened?" I was quick to ask.

"One semester," he began, "a freshman came to my dorm
office after about a week of school with a complaint. He
said he couldn't sleep in his current room and asked to be
moved. I never had gotten a request like that, and it piqued
my curiosity."

"We don't have any empty rooms. You're in that room by yourself, and I don't have anywhere to move you. What's wrong with your room?"

"I don't know how to tell you this," he began slowly. "But I can't sleep in that room. I think it's haunted. Every time I start to dose off, something wakes me up. I can feel an evil presence in the room. And I haven't slept in four days. I'm exhausted."

"I was dumbfounded. But I knew evil was real. I had just been taught that this sort of evil only happened in Bible times. So I went to my boss, a fine Christian man, and related the story and the problem. He was very understanding and sympathetic. He suggested we go to the young man's room that night, pray together about the problem, and anoint the door and window with oil, asking God to make it a place of peace and safety. So that's what we did. We did it in the wee hours of the morning darkness; and then—to celebrate the victory we were trusting God to perform—we cooked a big breakfast and ate it together. The boy slept fine every night from then on. The prayer and anointing of oil did the trick—but of course it was only a symbol of the faith we had in God's willingness and ability to protect us from all evil."

Lord, forgive me for thinking evil only existed and was active in years past. Remind me that Satan and his forces are still alive and active today, searching for opportunities to devour us or engulf us in fear and depression. Help others to claim the victory available to all who believe in Your Name. In Jesus's name, amen.

Bible-Based Thoughts Based on This Event:

Demons can be on Christian college campuses.
    Demons sometimes focus on harassment.
    Demons work best at nighttime.

Plagued by Many Demons

Jesus demanded, "What is your name?" "Legion," he replied, for *he was filled with many demons.* (Luke 8:30, NLT)

I have discovered that if you advertise a lecture series "Demons vs. Prayer," people from the community will come when they won't come for much of anything else. We did this in a small church in northern Louisiana and had some amazing results.

I noticed that a young lady on the third row was listening very intently to the lesson. A young man and two little girls sat with her. When I finished with the Sunday morning assembly presentation, she rushed over to me and hugged me, sobbing.

"Thank you for coming," came the tearful response. "I need help fighting my demons. You need to hear my story."

People were all around, waiting to talk, meet, or ask a question, so I said, "Do you want to call me or e-mail me so we can talk without so many people around?"

"Yes," she said. "Give me your card, and I'll get in touch with you tomorrow."

The next morning, I got the following *e-mail message* from her:

> I met you at church today. You gave me a hug, and I cried! I was at the church and heard your talk. I really felt like you were talking to me! I've been struggling with demons for a while now and feel like when I'm talking to God that the devil is always trying to jumble my words up! Maybe you can help me learn to overcome and fight my demons! I really feel like God put me in His house today just to hear you speak! Thank you so much for your words!

I quickly replied,

> Tell me the details of your story, and then we will talk on the phone.

> Where do I start?

Start at the beginning. Pretend we're just sitting together on a sofa, and tell me the whole story.

On April 27, 2005, my first child and only son, Christian, was born. He died twenty-seven hours later. That was the day my life changed. After his death, I turned to drugs to numb myself against the pain and depression. His father Joey and I buried him. The day before my son's funeral was the first time Joey hit me. After that, it got worse. On May 5, I married Joey. I felt that since we lost a child together we had to grieve together. We fought all the time. It was horrible. I had my second child, Olivia, on May 22, 2006. I was clean from drugs while I was pregnant with her. The abuse from Joey continued. I left Joey a few times but went back because I thought he would change. Didn't happen. Abuse got worse every time. On June 13, 2007, I had my third child, Kat Lyn. I was clean when I was pregnant with her also. Joey is not her father, but he signed the birth certificate. I left Joey for good on May 5, 2009. It was me and my baby girls against the world! But I started using drugs again. I've done just about all kinds, sad to say. I fell deep into drugs at this time. I finally gave temporary custody to my mom and lived a fast life. Then I cleaned up and moved away. I was doing good but had a boyfriend who wasn't the right guy. After a bad breakup in April 2012, I started using meth and heroin by needles. I knew I had a problem. I called my mom and told her what was happening, and she helped me get into rehab. I checked in on 7/30/12. Best thing that's ever happened for me. Saved my life! I was dead walking in! I left rehab and have not touched or been around meth or heroin since! I stopped talking to my old friends and moved completely away!

In August 2012, Jay (my boyfriend) and I became a couple and started living like a family! He is the best thing that's ever happened to my daughters and me! He makes me happy and helps me stay sober, a true blessing!

God has opened many doors for me, but I still feel the devil holding me back. I've been attending beauty school since January, and it's my dream come true! I've been sober for almost two years, raising my daughters and being a real momma! Learning to love and trust again with Jay. I know I've been blessed beyond measure, and I'm thankful for all my trials, tribulations, and blessings. But the devil still bothers me! A lot!

After hearing you at church Sunday, I deleted all the pornography from my phone! I've started praying and telling God how much I need and love Him. I know that God made our paths cross! I want a closer relationship with God! I want to walk, talk, and live in His spirit! I've tried to do this on my own but never felt I was doing it "right."

Wow. What a story. God is definitely at work in your life. I can't tell you how to fight your demons, but I can tell you how to make them leave. But I need a little more information. Tell me all about your conversion experience. Why were you baptized? And are you legally married to Jay?

What do you mean by conversion? I got baptized because I grew up in church, and it was expected. I don't guess I did it for the right reasons. My first husband, Joey, committed suicide. Jay and I aren't married, but we plan to. He is currently going through a divorce. Also, we want to wait a few years until the time is right. We've both been through a lot.

Okay. Good. That's what I needed to know to help you with this…

Being baptized because of peer pressure won't help you. It must be your own decision, and to be in covenant with God through Christ. If you don't have faith in Jesus as Lord and really understand all that, it's really just getting wet. I hope that doesn't sound like criticism. I'm just trying to help. Once you are in covenant with God through Christ, you have access to His power and His strength. This gives you the power to command demons to leave and stay gone—in Jesus's name.

"Peter said to them, '*Change your hearts and lives and be baptized*, each one of you, in the name of Jesus Christ. Then God will forgive your sins, *and you will receive the gift of the Holy Spirit*'" (Acts 2:38, ERV).

But you have another important issue. You can't be in covenant with God and continue living together without being married. It nullifies your power—rendering you helpless against the demons. Does that make sense? Love without obedience isn't good enough. Having ongoing sexual relations with a man you aren't married to is called fornication or sexual sin, and it steals all your power. Do you understand? The preacher there can help you with this if you like. I live too far away.

"And as they were eating, *Jesus* took bread, blessed and broke it, and gave it to the disciples and said, 'Take, eat; this is My body.' Then He *took the cup*, and gave thanks, *and gave it to them, saying*, 'Drink from it, all of you. *For this is My blood of the new covenant, which is shed for many for the remission of sins*'" (Matt. 26:26–28, NKJV).

Are you willing to submit to God's rules so you can permanently eliminate your demons? If not, I am powerless to help you.

Okay! I get the baptized deal. But the sexual sin part made me sick! I know it's not in God's will, but does it really mean that Jay and I can't be together?

All I can do is tell you the truth of what the Bible says. Sex outside of marriage is never acceptable to God. It doesn't have to be a big fancy wedding. It's just has to be legal where you live. God also put the leaders in power. Just marry him. I can't make you do anything, but based on the Bible, you shouldn't have sex again until you are legally married.

"So *run away from sexual sin*. Every other sin people do is outside their bodies, but *those who sin sexually sin against their own bodies*" (1 Cor. 6:18, NCV).

I love you. And God loves you. I can tell you want to do the right thing. Explain it to Jay and help him understand your desire to please God.

We do want to be married. I talked to him about this last night, and he understands. He was in church before his divorce. He says that life and God made more sense when he was married. So he knows where my heart is, and he understands my need to be closer to God. I want to be baptized. Is that even an option? And would it even matter?

Terrific! I am so glad Jay understands. You and Jay can only grow together with God's blessing as a married couple! Yes! Baptism is an option. Call the preacher there. He will be glad to help you. In fact, I will call him for you and give him your phone number. And it definitely would matter. Greatly.

We can't get married yet because his divorce is complicated. But thank you for all of your words and advice and prayers! Please don't give up on me. I want a closer relationship with God, and I want to live in his glory! I know I've got a lot of work to do, but I know I can do it!

I understand, but you need to handle this as quickly as possible. Sin is sin, and there are no excuses in God's eyes for having sex with someone whom you aren't married to yet. If you're not sure you want to marry him, then you should not have sex with him. I hope that doesn't sound mean or unkind. It's just practical truth. God knows what's in your heart, but He still expects obedience to His laws and commandments—including premarital sex. You can be forgiven and clean in God's sight from all your past sins.

"Don't you know that wicked people won't inherit God's kingdom? Stop deceiving yourselves! *People who continue to commit sexual sins*, who worship false gods, those who commit adultery, homosexuals, or thieves, those who are greedy or drunk, who use abusive language, or who rob people *will not inherit God's kingdom.* That's what some of you were! *But you have been washed and made holy, and you have received God's approval* in the name of the Lord Jesus Christ and in the Spirit of our God" (1 Cor. 6:9–11, GWT)

I have talked to Jay, and I do want to marry him, and he wants to marry me! You have given me a lot to think and pray about! Thanks so much!

I'm happy to help.

Two weeks later, the minister there called and told me the good news: the newlyweds were baptized.

Are their troubles over? No.

But will they have access to God's power now? Yes. And they can bind the demons in Jesus's name and send them to the pit.

Lord, thank You for helping this couple see the wisdom of Your eternal truths. Many other couples are in the same position: confused, afraid, and demonized. Lead them to the help they need, and give them a willing heart to do what it takes to get into a right relationship with You. Thank You for making that possible. In Jesus's name, amen.

Bible-Based Thoughts Based on This Event:

Demonized people already know demons are real.

Demons can help blind you to your own disobedience.

Demonized people are looking for something that offers hope.

Demons don't care if you are baptized, as long as you don't believe.

Demons want you to be sexually active, living in immorality.

Demons can confuse people who are trying to pray to God.

Demons often attack when people are at their weakest.
Demons can use your grief to distance you from God.
Demons can work through your personal porn.
Demons often promote spousal abuse.
Demons can promote suicide.

Two Thousand Pigs

> Then Jesus demanded, "What is your name?" And he replied, "My name is Legion, because there are many of us inside this man." Then the evil spirits begged him again and again not to send them to some distant place. (Mark 5:9–10, NLT)

In Mark 5, Jesus meets a man possessed by many demons. He lived in a cemetery, which is strange, to say the least. The locals had tried to chain him up, but the demon-possessed man had great strength and simply snapped the chains. He was out of control. He mutilated himself with many cuts on a regular basis. He even howled like a wolf. I'm sure he instilled great fear in the hearts of the nearby people.

When he saw Jesus, he screamed and called Him God's Son as he begged not to be tortured. This demonstrates a submissive spirit to Jesus in the area of authority:

> When Jesus was still some distance away, the man saw him, ran to meet him, and bowed low before him. *With a shriek, he screamed, "Why are you interfering with me, Jesus, Son of the Most High God? In the name of God, I beg you, don't torture me!"* (Mark 5:6–7, NLT)

Jesus spoke to the demons, not the man. He asked for a name, and the demon in charge immediately told him there were many demons there. Notice then that they begged again and again not to leave. Have you ever wondered why?

I have often wondered about this since Jews don't eat pork. And this wasn't a small pig farm. There were two thousand pigs there (Mark 5:13).

Perry Stone writes in his book *Purging Your House, Pruning Your Family Tree*, that he learned from a tour guide in Israel that there was an ancient temple to the Greek god Zeus very near to that graveyard. Pigs were used as a sacrifice to Zeus. Perry connected the dots—the demons were likely asking to (a) stay close to their liege, Zeus, and (b) they would be involved in worship to Zeus by being in the living tissue of the pigs that would eventually be sacrificed to him.

But it wasn't to be. When Jesus gave them permission to enter the pigs (at their own request), the herd of hogs headed for the water and drowned, thus rendering the demonic plans null and void:

> "*Send us into those pigs the spirits begged.* Let us enter them." So *Jesus gave them permission.* The evil spirits came out of the man and entered the pigs, and the entire herd *of about 2,000 pigs plunged down the steep hillside into the lake and drowned in the water.* (Mark 5:12–13, NLT)

More and more, I'm beginning to realize how much spiritual warfare is smoldering right below the surface in many Bible stories.

Lord, open my eyes to all the ways Satan is involved all around me in today's world. And help me to know what I can do about it. In Jesus's name, amen.

Bible-Based Thoughts Based on This Event:

Demons enjoy living near the dead.
  Demons want to be involved in idolatry.
  Demons enjoy inflicting pain on their host.
  Demons are subject to the authority of Jesus Christ.
  Demons like to inhabit living beings—both human and animal.

Chip Goes Camping…for God

> *During the night God spoke to him in a vision.* "Jacob! Jacob!" he called.

> "Here I am," Jacob replied. (Gen. 46:2, NLT)

God is continually opening my eyes to the spiritual world. In fact, I have an interesting story to share with you…

Chip was a young man in his lower thirties. One summer, he had an accident that injured his leg. During his recovery, he became addicted to painkillers. After the refills ran out, he did the unthinkable, forging the doctor's signature to get more pills. He told me face-to-face, "Steve, I would have traded my family for a handful of pills."

Shortly before this all caught up with him, a friend found Chip's Bible that he had left in the pew at church. He saw that it was Chip's, and as he picked it up, he got a "weird feeling" that something was wrong with Chip. He immediately got in his car and drove to Chip's house to ask what was wrong. Chip proceeded to explain the whole story of exactly what *was* wrong, and that he would soon be indicted.

Chip *was* indicted soon after that, and he went forward at the end of a morning worship assembly, confessing sin and asking for the prayers of the congregation. He received over two hundred and fifty cards and notes of encouragement and quite a few phone calls saying, "I have had the same problem." (From people you would least expect to hear that.) The overwhelming response of love and understanding gave him a false sense of security. Chip *thought* he had his addiction whipped at this time, but he didn't.

He got an *extremely light* sentence. Probation meant that if he kept clean and reported properly, the incident wouldn't even go in his record. But it was not to be. Chip violated his probation. At this point, he realized that it was only a matter of time before it caught up with him—again.

Realizing he needed professional help to kick his habit, he checked himself into a nearby addiction hospital.

Chip was very nervous about going through the program, because he was sure that he was mainly going to encounter a group of long-haired hippie-type bikers. And that's exactly what happened. He finally worked up the courage to meet the group of "hippies" and was surprised to become good friends with one of them. He had hair down to the middle of his back and worked on an assembly line. Chip discovered that he was very intelligent, with an IQ of over 170, and was doing a lot of reading—especially the Bible. Chip ended up converting and baptizing this man. Chip said the guy "wouldn't fit into any church" but was holding services for other "bikers" in his home each week. Chip had the weirdest feeling about the whole experience, because this was a type of guy that he wouldn't even have *associated* with at home.

Soon after this, Chip went on a camping trip and again found himself making friends with people he wouldn't even have associated with at home.

On the return from this trip, Chip was traveling on an interstate highway and passed several hitchhikers. Strangely, he found himself pulling over to pick up another "hippie." This guy had long hair and a dirty backpack. As he got in with Chip, he opened up a Bible and began to discuss God. As they got near a city, he said, "Chip, my water bottle is empty. Would you stop at one of the local restaurants and refill it for me? They won't let me in because of how I look." Chip said, "Sure. Do you have any food?" He said no. "Do you have any money?" Again, he said no. Chip said, "How do you survive?" The guy said, "God provides for me every day." When Chip got back into the car and handed the man the full bottle, the man said, "If you give someone a drink of water in my name, you will not lose your reward in heaven." He quoted the verse where Jesus makes that statement. This took Chip by complete surprise.

As they traveled on, the guy finally said, "Oh, Chip, I need out right here." Chip said, "Oh, okay," and pulled over to let him out. As Chip was pulling away, it dawned on him that he was in the middle of nowhere, and he looked into his rearview mirror. The "hippie" was already "thumbing a ride" with someone else, sort of like "I'm through with you, Chip. I have somewhere else to be now."

All Chip could think about was this: he has no money and no food, and God provides for him every day.

As Chip pulled away from the drop-off spot, he looked in his rearview mirror. The man had vanished. Although the terrain was flat, Chip couldn't see him anywhere.

> Don't forget *to show hospitality to strangers, for some who have done this have entertained angels* without realizing it! (Heb. 13:2, NLT)

A short time before Labor Day weekend (with a Monday holiday), Chip had a dream. He *vividly* remembered every detail when he woke in the morning. And he had the *same dream three nights in a row*. In fact, the details were so numerous and so vivid that he decided to sit down and write them out. It was eleven pages handwritten.

He was supposed to go back camping at a certain State Park. He was to hand out pamphlets on addiction. He was to go alone. He was to take no food and no money (God would provide). He was to counsel others with addiction problems. He was to take many different changes of clothes because of all the different people he would be talking to. He was to leave on the trip on the day of the new moon. He didn't even know when that was, but when he looked at the calendar, he discovered that it was on the Wednesday before the Labor Day weekend holiday. He was to return on the day that "men celebrate their labor," Labor Day Monday.

Chip shared his dream with just a few people and decided he would go. He even went to a copy shop to reproduce handouts on addiction.

Interestingly enough, this particular Wednesday just happened to be the day that his church began forty days of prayer that started with a forty-hour fast. Chip didn't even know about the fast, but he observed it "accidentally" because he left with "no food and no money" and did not get a meal until Thursday evening.

Hurricane Fran had just come through, and the camping area was pelted with rain. Chip got his camp set up on Wednesday evening. On Thursday morning, he left his tent to hand out all these pamphlets on addiction he had printed and brought with him. It was misting rain, quite bad weather. It was also in the middle of the week, and there was no one there with which to share the brochures. All he could think was, *What am I doing here?*

He decided to walk to all the different camping areas, looking for someone with which to share the information. Finally, in a remote camping area, he found one tent off by itself. He started toward the tent and decided to yell that he was coming their way so he wouldn't startle the people in the tent. He yelled, "Hey, I am handing out these pamphlets on addiction, and I just want to give you one." From inside the tent, a voice yelled back, "Get out of here!" Chip responded, "Okay, but I just need to give you this first. I'll just slide it under the door. If you decide you want to talk, I am camped in a tent about a hundred yards to the west of you." The man responded with, "Leave me alone!"

Chip left and went back to his tent. There was literally no one else to hand the pamphlets out to.

About twenty minutes later, the man showed up at Chip's tent and said, "Hey, I need to talk." Chip unzipped his tent and came out. It had stopped raining by this time, so they sat down together at a picnic table and began to talk. The man had a fanny pouch on, and as he unzipped it, he said, "I want you to hold something for me." He handed Chip a loaded pistol. He said, "Chip, when you yelled at me in the tent, I had this gun in my mouth and was ready to pull the trigger. I am a Church of Christ preacher, and I am addicted to alcohol. I can't shake the habit. I was ready to give up."

Chip had been a Church of Christ preacher earlier in his life in a small town for about two years. Who better to council a Church of Christ preacher with an addiction than an ex-Church of Christ preacher who had just finished an addiction program? No one. Only God could do that.

Chip talked to him for two days and then took him home. He helped the man share his secret with his wife.

He had hidden his addiction so well that his wife didn't even know.

Chip encouraged him to share the problem with at least one of his elders. He indicated that there was one man he could share it with, so they drove over to his house. It was a seventy-year-old man, and Chip was thinking, "*This* is the one we are going to share this with?" They told him the whole story, and the elder responded with, "I had the same problem twenty years ago. Nobody knew it."

Chip spent the night at the preacher's home and taught a Bible class the next day at his church on addiction, using another of the several changes of clothes he had brought. That afternoon, he drove the man to an addiction hospital and got him checked in. Finally, on Monday, he came home: the day "men celebrate their labor."

Lord, thank You for using Chip to save another man's life. Use me to Your glory. Give me a willing heart and an able body. In Jesus's name, amen.

Bible-Based Thoughts Based on This Event:

God can still use dreams if He wants to; He's God.

God can use the bad things you experience to help others.

Following God can sometimes seem like a strange journey.

Demons promote discouragement, depression, and suicide.

Everyone has something in their past they aren't proud of.

If God is trying to get someone's attention and you keep bailing them out,

God will go through you to get to them if He has to.

Sharing Chip's Story

But the believers who were scattered preached the Good News about Jesus wherever they went. (Acts 8:4, NLT)

I shared that story with Bible classes and with various friends, giving God the praise and glory. Be warned: when you actively spread great stories about God's power, you just moved way up Satan's target list.

Soon after sharing this God story, I sat down with the woman who paid the bills at my office. As we reviewed our balance, bills, and other upcoming expenses, I realized that it was overwhelming. In fact, I was convinced that we would have to borrow a substantial amount to meet these obligations.

When I went back to my office, I immediately had the thought, *This is a satanic attack. Satan is mad that I'm sharing*

Chip's story. I quickly bowed my head and prayed, "God, this is more than I can handle. Please help me through this crisis."

Within thirty minutes, the phone rang. It was a Christian friend I had not seen or heard from for a long time. He said, "Steve, I just got this uncontrollable urge to pray for you, and I don't know what to pray for. What is going on in your life?" I shared Chip's story with him, along with my cash flow problems. He responded with, "That's what I needed to know. I'll be praying about that."

Right away, things started falling into place that solved the problem. In seven days, we went from $75,000 in the red to $25,000 in the black. In my fifteen years in business at this point, I had never seen that happen before.

Lord, give me the boldness to keep sharing stories that bring You glory. Remind me that You are bigger than any problem I face—seen or unseen. In Jesus's name, amen.

Bible-Based Thoughts Based on This Event:

Satan and his demons want you to focus on your fears.

It's wise to pray and turn to God when faced with a great difficulty.

God often nudges people to pray for you when your need is great.

God can turn your financial situation around in record time.

Home for Unwed Mothers

Just as *you cannot understand* the path of the wind or *the mystery of a tiny baby growing in its mother's womb*, so *you cannot understand the activity of God, who does all things.* (Eccles. 11:5, NLT)

Word spread about the stakes, and I began to get calls from people who wanted to come by to pick some up or hear more about them in general. One such call came from a nearby organization that helps unwed mothers. It's a place where women can go with their baby when they have nowhere else to go. But it's also a place to retool, retrain, and refocus so their future can be better than their past. They are required to contribute daily in a work rotation schedule of chores, continue their education (usually on-line), and do community volunteer work to help others. They also have Bible studies daily in which they are required to participate.

They had heard about the stakes from someone I knew in the community, so I met with the director and the manager of the organization for a quick lunch. I told them many of the stories, and they loved the idea.

"We love that idea," the director exclaimed. "We want to stake out our facility!"

So they did. A few weeks later, they told me what they did.

They turned it into a ceremony of sorts. Everyone went outside to the first corner of the property. The stake sets have different verses on each stake (future ones will soon have all seventeen passages on every stake). The group included the directors, the staff, the residents, and even the babies. I mention this because I have begun to notice that the more people involved in the staking process, the more effective it seems to be. This is especially true if those with the highest authority over that property are involved. Because of this, I think it's even better if the elders of a church, for example, take the lead in a ceremony like this and promote this as an act of faith that will affect everyone positively.

As this diverse group gathered at the location for the first stake to be placed, the director explained they were claiming this land for God, dedicating it to His service and glory. They read the first set of verses out loud as everyone listened, and then the director hammered the stake all the way into the ground so that it was completely out of sight. They repeated this process at all four corners, ending the ceremony with a dedication prayer as a final punctuation point.

Interesting things started to happen right away.

One of their "star pupils," so to speak, was a girl who was doing great in the program. She was turning her life around. She had almost completed her GED so she could qualify for a better job. She immediately marched up to the director and said, "I can't stay here anymore." She got her stuff and her baby, and she left. And she had nowhere to go. They later discovered why. She was still doing drugs. I've noticed on some occasions that when a place is staked out, if someone there is actively involved in evil, they can't stand to be inside the stakes on land that's been claimed for God.

A short time later, they asked me to come teach their 9:00 p.m. Wednesday night Bible study. This gives the moms a chance to get their babies in bed and then be able to focus on the study. They bring their Bibles and gather in a large meeting room. They introduced me as "The Stake Guy," which is often the case nowadays.

"This is the guy," the director intoned, "who came up with the idea for the stakes that we put out the other day. Go ahead, Steve. Tell them your stories!"

So I began. I told them many of the stories you've just read along with many of the verses discussed in this book. After about an hour—during a short pause as I was winding down—I heard one of the ladies say under her breath, "This makes perfect sense."

"What does?" I asked.

"Oh. Sorry," she replied. "I was just thinking out loud how this makes sense because we were all fussing and fighting and arguing over every little thing until we staked this place out. That all stopped."

"Really?"

"Yes," another woman responded. "And I was having nightmares every single night until we staked it out too."

"Wow."

Then a shy girl in the corner sitting on the floor spoke up. "You won't believe this," she started. "I was sitting on the porch the very next day after we staked it out, and this man came walking down the street by our facility. He was just evil. I could feel it in the air, and you could almost see it on him as he approached. As he got closer, he noticed me there in the shade of the small porch, and he started talking to me. But I couldn't respond. I was scared to death—too afraid to speak. This angered him as he got closer and continued to talk to me as I just stared. There was a pretty wide area between us, and he started to step up onto our property here toward me. I stared in shock as he lifted his leg to come closer, and he froze in midair—one foot on the ground and the other lifted up, still in the air. He got a funny look on his face. He backed up and moved over a little. Same result. He tried a third time, but he was literally unable to come closer, like there was an invisible wall holding him back. That's when I realized that he had reached the imaginary line between the stakes we had just placed. The man turned and left without saying another word.

Folks, I can't make this stuff up. I don't really understand it, except to say that God's word is still powerful. He's still the great "I Am," not the "I Used to Could."

Lord, I praise You as the all-powerful One. None can stand against you. Deliver me from evil. Protect me and my house from those who want to cause harm in any way. Open my eyes, ears, heart, and mind so I can discern and avoid and conquer the evil beings who target me, my family, my ministry, and my church. In Jesus's name, amen.

Bible-Based Thoughts Based on This Event:

Demons are especially affected adversely when authority figures place the stakes.

Demons are expelled from tracts of land that have been dedicated to God's service.

Demons may somehow be connected to nightmares, night terrors, and bad dreams.

Demons work to cause strife and dissension among groups of people and individuals.

Demons may be attached to some people, making those folks uneasy near God's word.

Water in the Apartments

At your command, the water fled; at the sound of your
thunder, *it hurried away.* (Ps. 104:7, NLT)

One of the staff members at the home for unwed mothers got some stakes and took them home to her apartment.
She stood them in the four corners of the place and prayed
for God's divine protection.

The next Saturday around 9:00 a.m., she got a knock on
the door—an unusual thing for a Saturday morning. When
she answered the door, it was the building supervisor.

"Can I help you?" she asked.

"I'm just here to inspect your water damage," he said. He
seemed exasperated.

"What water damage?" she replied.

"Well," he explained impatiently, "the guy right next
door to you went crazy and flooded the whole building."

"You are welcome to come and look," she stated. "But
God has been protecting my apartment."

There wasn't one drop of water anywhere inside her place.
And to make it even more stunning, she shared a kitchen
wall and a bathroom wall with the man who flooded the
building. Her apartment should have been the first place
the water invaded. But it didn't. Not a drop. God is still on
the throne, and prayer still works.

Lord, Your word still has power. Thank You for reminding me of that fact. When my faith is weak and all seems hopeless, please remind me again. In Jesus's name, amen.

River Water Rising

> The Red Sea saw them coming and hurried out of their way! The water of the Jordan River turned away. (Ps. 114:3, NLT)

One of my speaking trips took me to West Texas. A few months after the event, that area was dealing with storm after storm that dumped an enormous amount of rain in the area. The main water source for the area was a large lake that had dropped to dangerously low levels as a result of the Texas drought in recent years, so the rains were actually quite welcome. However, when massive amounts fall in a short time period, flooding is often an unwanted side effect.

This was the case for my friend Dee. Dee and her husband had purchased a set of stakes from me at the area event several months earlier but hadn't yet put them on the corners of their business property, which was right on the river.

Broadcast news and weather reports warned of rising waters and recommended evacuation. They began to worry and fret—and pray.

That's when they remembered the stakes. The waters were rising as they began to put them out. West Texas floods can often rise very rapidly. When the final stake was installed, water was lapping at a critical point. But as soon as they said, "Amen," and ended their prayer following the installation of all four stakes, the waters began receding. Only God can do that. He is still on the throne, and prayer still works.

Lord, creation came into being at the sound of Your command, and Your word is just as powerful now as it was then. We give you all glory and honor. In Jesus's name, amen.

Divorce House

> Yes, and the Lord will *deliver me from every evil attack* and will bring me safely into his heavenly Kingdom. All glory to God forever and ever! Amen. (2 Tim. 4:18, NLT)

I got a call from a church leader in North Arkansas. I had helped with an outreach a couple of years prior to this, and he knew I was working on a new book on the topic of spiritual warfare.

I have noticed that when I talk about the subjects of demons and spiritual warfare, people will tell me stories they don't usually share and ask me for advice about unusual things—things they don't normally talk about.

Don's question was unique, focused on the battle of good and evil, and specific in nature: "Steve," he began, "I live sort of out in the country on a small piece of property, and my daughter just bought the house next door on a piece of property similar in size to mine. They got a great deal on the house, and we're excited to have them next door, but I'm worried about the house. The last three families who lived there got a divorce. I don't want that to happen to my daughter. What do I do to clean up the property from evil?"

What would you say?

I didn't even hesitate. So many folks had been calling me with exciting results from putting stakes around their homes and properties that I couldn't wait to share that idea with Don. I explained what they were, what to do, and the fact that it wasn't a magic formula—just a symbol of their faith in God's promise to protect his people from evil (part of the Lord's Prayer).

> And do not lead us into temptation, but *deliver us from the evil one.* For Yours is the kingdom and the power and the glory forever. Amen. (Matt. 6:13, NKJV)

"Send me three sets of stakes as soon as you can," said Don. So I did.

I didn't hear from Don until the first week of January, about a month later.

"Steve," he began, "I have a story for you." I couldn't wait to hear about his results.

"We got the stakes in the mail on a Saturday. Sunday afternoon we put them out. First, I put one set of stakes around my own house, praying the verses that were etched in the thermal labels on the fiberglass stakes designed to last outdoors."

"Then I put a set around my daughter's new house, even praying in every room of their new home."

"I put the final set around the borders of our adjoining properties."

"With the stakes in place and all the prayers uttered, I went to bed around 10:00 p.m. peaceful and satisfied. It was now in the Lord's hands."

"I woke up with quite a start just a little bit after midnight. I could hear someone running back and forth across the roof. I grabbed my shotgun and a floodlight and headed out the door. But there was nothing you could see—with the human eye. So I went back inside the house, fully perplexed. Then I heard it again, and I instantly knew what it was. I hit my knees in prayer. A furious demon was running, jumping, and savagely scratching on the walls, the roof, the vent pipes, and the windows. It went on for about four hours, and I prayed the entire time. I returned to the yard twice more during this stretch of time, searching the roof with the light, gun at the ready. Never saw anything. But the noise—like a person running on the outside of my walls and roof—was quite unnerving. Round and round my house it went. Evil noises around me and prayers going up, all at the same time."

> But you belong to God, my dear children. You have already won a victory over those people, because *the Spirit who lives in you is greater than the spirit who lives in the world.* (1 John 4:4, NLT)

"At 4:30 a.m., it stopped, and everything was silent. I was exhausted, but quite relieved."

"That was over a month ago," he said, and we haven't heard a thing since. I figure that whatever we expelled from the house next door tried to get into mine, but the Bible stakes prevented it."

Lord, thank You for the power available to us through our covenant relationship with You. When fear starts to grip me, remind me that Your Spirit in me is greater than anything or anyone I will ever face. In Jesus's name, amen.

Bible-Based Thoughts Based on This Event:

Demons can be territorial.

   Demons often work to promote divorce.

   Demons may return to their territorial assignment at nighttime.

   Demons can't return after fervent prayer and the posting of Scriptures.

   Demons may attack those who have disturbed their boundaries.

Suicide House

> When his armor-bearer saw that *Saul* was dead, he also *fell on his sword and died.* (1 Chron. 10:5, AMP)

> Then *Judas* threw the silver coins down in the Temple and *went out and hanged himself.* (Matt. 27:5, NLT)

He lived right around the corner from us. He was a senior in high school. He was active and well liked. He had numerous friends, and he participated in many school activities. Everything looked fine on the outside. His parents had no clue that he was terribly upset on the inside. He was blaming himself for his problems. It may have been a tiff with a girl, a bad grade, or an issue with a friend.

His problems seemed bigger than he could handle, and he was convinced that everyone would be better if he were dead (that's how Satan works). So he shot himself in his own bedroom.

Soon, his parents couldn't stand living in the house where their only child killed himself, so they put it up for sale. The family who bought the house had two sons, and one of them was now sleeping in the same bedroom where the young man from the previous family had committed suicide.

Six months later, this boy confessed to his youth group that he needed prayer because he now had thoughts of suicide. A while later, he actually did attempt it. He took a bottle of pills to end it all—but got scared and called his mom. She rushed home from work and took him to the emergency room. They pumped his stomach and saved his life. With that thought in mind, I offer this prayer:

Lord, I dedicate my house to Your glory. I pledge to use my life and my assets to help further Your kingdom in every possible way. So anything evil in my home—visible or invisible—I command in the name of Jesus Christ to be bound in chains and put in the pit, awaiting judgment, so they can't hurt others in the future. In Jesus's name, amen.

Suicide House Follow-up

> *Those who respect the Lord* will have security, and *their children will be protected.* (Prov. 14:26, NCV)

While I was writing this book, I was out for a walk one day and went right by this particular house. There was a moving truck there, and the family who now owned it was moving out. Although I felt quite awkward, I was compelled to stop and ask the owner if they had experienced anything strange while living there.

I was careful in how I introduced myself and asked about it:

"Can I ask you a strange question?" I began. "I live right around the corner."

"Sure," he responded kindly.

"I'm a Christian author, and I used to know the family who lived there. The previous owner (before them) had a son to commit suicide there, and their own son ended up attempting suicide too. I teach on demons and spiritual warfare, and I was just wondering if you guys had anything unusual happen too."

"Yes," he quickly said, "our son had terrible night terrors while we lived here—worse than we've ever experienced."

Lord, open our eyes and minds so we can connect the dots and understand how Satan is at work in our daily lives so we can pray more effectively. In Jesus's name, amen.

Bible-Based Thoughts Based on This Event:

Demons often focus on the young; both parents not affected here.

Demons may sometimes promote depression that can lead to suicide.

Demons can be territorial, inflicting the same malady on each new person.

Daddy's Little Girl

A Gentile woman who lived there came to him, pleading, "Have mercy on me, O Lord, Son of David! For *my daughter is possessed by a demon that torments her severely.*" (Matt. 15:22, NLT)

I was recently invited to speak at a men's conference designed to encourage those dedicated to serving in church leadership. There were about two hundred in attendance from two states and about fifty churches. It was a great honor. I was one of only two speakers on the program of this all-day event. I spent the first session sharing the exciting things I found in the Bible about heaven, which led to my first book, *My Search for the Real Heaven*, and the second on thoughts from my newest release, *My Search for Prayers Satan Hates*.

In all my travels, I have never charged anyone a speaking fee. Don't get me wrong—I don't turn down money. I have bills like everyone else. But I have never charged, and I never know when I accept an invitation to come speak whether they are going to pay me or not, or even whether they will help with expenses. I just made the decision long ago to simply trust that God will take care of that stuff. I just ask if I can set up a table with my resource materials in the back and make them available to anyone interested. It always seems to work out. It's all about faith, right?

It was no different at this event. I had a small table set up in the foyer and went there to greet folks after I was finished. I love people and was busy meeting many of them in the lobby when a tall, shy-acting man slipped up quietly and stood patiently nearby. When I had a short break, he slipped up and introduced himself, asking to speak privately when the event was over. I readily agreed and instructed him to hang around so we could be alone for a visit. He did.

"I need to tell you about my daughter," he began. "We have three children, and she is the oldest. Our children don't attend public school; we home school them. She is ten years old now, but she was only seven when her personality suddenly changed—for the worse. She started saying things that were mean, ugly, even sinister. She might say to her brother, 'I'm going to take a knife and cut you,' and to her sister, 'I'm going to burn you.' She even said, 'I'm going to kill you.' We were all shocked since she had never talked like that. And where were these evil ideas coming from? From a school called home!"

"We sat her down and began to question her," he continued. "It took time, patience, and focused questioning. But she finally said something about those words coming from 'Legba.' 'Who is "Legba"?' we asked. And she finally explained that Legba was the one who came and sat at the foot of her bed every night, watching her while she slept. Obviously, we were shocked and terrified to hear this. It was demonic. We didn't know who to tell—or much less—what to do. Would people think we were crazy?"

They were desperate. And they felt infinitely unqualified to remedy the situation. They finally decided to share the problem with their minister. He was very kind and understanding and had just read my book on demons, prayer, and spiritual warfare, *My Search for Prayers Satan Hates*. So they laid hands on the girl and prayed about this whole situation.

"Things definitely got better," he told me. That had been three years ago when the little girl was about seven. "But there still times we have been worried."

"How are things now?" I asked. "Okay," he said, but there are still problems, and it seems to have been getting a little worse lately. I love your idea of staking out the property with tent stakes covered in Bible verses, but I don't have any money to buy them."

"Here," I said, handing him a set. "They are free to you. Let me know how it goes."

He thanked me, and we parted.

The next morning after I spoke in a Bible class and in their worship service, I met his wife and the little girl. The girl came up while her mother and I were talking and rudely interrupted with some petty complaint. Her mother—in a rather irritated fashion—reminded her that she was the mom and that she was busy talking. The girl obeyed but was obviously angry about something.

I thought a lot about this girl and Legba on my return home. Children are innocent. Children trust. And children are inquisitive. I wondered what the girl thought when she saw someone (or something) at the foot of her bed the first time. How do children usually respond? She might sit up and say, "What's your name?" And she probably did. And how might the demons respond in an effort to gain her trust? "My name is Legba. What's your name?"

I went on home Sunday afternoon and went to bed early after such an eventful weekend. I was very tired.

But I awoke suddenly in the middle of the night and sat up in bed. I had been dreaming and realized that I needed to call the little girl's father and get him to ask her three questions. I didn't hear an audible voice, and I wasn't at all afraid. I can't explain it. I just knew I had to get him to do that.

The one other time this had happened in my life I had been praying about how to put my heaven book together, deciding on the chapter titles and the order the information should be presented in. I felt completely unqualified to organize and write a book, so I prayed for God to help me get things in the right order. One night at three in the morning, I woke up. It was like I was listening to a recording of a long list of very specific things. I listened, it finished, and I started to doze off. It started over. I listened again, it finished again, and I started to doze again. When it began the third time, I realized I needed to get up and write it down. It was a list of the titles of the chapters and the order I needed to put them.

I realized in this case that I needed to call the man the next day and get him to ask his daughter three specific questions. But I was very sleepy and very tired from the weekend trip; so, although I had never done this before, I said, "Lord, I'm really tired. I promise I'll do this tomorrow if you will just remind me, okay?" Looking back, I can't believe I did that to the Lord of the universe, but I did. I talk to Him now like He's my best friend. Then I lay back down in the bed and went to sleep.

The next morning when I awoke, I had no memory of the dream. I ate breakfast and went straight to the hospital because a friend was having surgery. I prayed with them and then sat in the waiting room with the family and friends waiting for the report from the doctor. I was there most of the morning, and my friend's prognosis was excellent. (Prayer still works.)

When I finally sat down at my computer, it was about noon. I had no sooner sat down before I remembered my dream and felt a sense of urgency to call the father and get him to ask the girl three questions. I reached for a blank piece of paper and said out loud, "What were the questions?"

I had just gotten my pen and paper ready and uttered those words, and the three questions immediately came to me:

1. Did Legba touch her?
2. Did Legba give her anything?
3. Did Legba introduce her to anyone?

I got the father's number from the minister at his church. It was a little after noon when I dialed their home phone number. He picked up on the first ring.

"I had a dream last night," I quickly explained. "God gave me three very specific questions you need to ask your daughter. Please get a pen to write them down word for word." He did and said they would ask her immediately and call me right back.

Five minutes later, my phone rang, and it was the dad. "We asked her the questions just as you instructed," he began. "Legba didn't ever touch her or give her anything, but when we asked if he introduced to her anyone, she said, 'Yes. All his friends.'"

"That's not good," I said. "She's talking about other demons."

"That's not all," the father continued. "She also said that Legba invited her to go with him to 'Funland.'"

"What's 'Funland'?" we asked.

"I don't know," the girl responded. "I never went. But I thought it was something like an amusement park."

Then we asked her, "Honey, do you remember when the preacher came over and prayed with you about all this?"

"Yes," she quickly said, "and after that prayer, Legba couldn't talk anymore. He still came and sat at the foot of my bed every night to watch me sleep, but he couldn't speak."

"Did he ever leave?" the dad asked.

"Yes," answered the girl. "One night I realized that since he couldn't talk to me anymore he was going to start talking to my little sister in the other bed. That made me mad, so I sat up and said, 'No. Leave my sister alone. You need to go now.' And that's when he finally left."

Notice that the demon left when the little girl got angry and told him to go.

After hearing this additional information, I knew they needed to ask the girl one more question. "Write this down," I told the father. "There's one more question you need to ask her. Be sure to word it exactly as I relate it to you: is there a magic word or secret way she can always go to Funland?"

"I'll call you right back," came the fatherly reply.

Five minutes later, he called right back.

"We asked her exactly as you instructed: 'Is there a magic word or secret way you can always go to Funland?'"

When we asked her this question, she looked down at the floor for a very long time. We waited patiently, giving her space, but determined to get the answer. Finally, she looked up and said with fear on her face, "Yes, Daddy, but I'm not allowed to tell you."

Why would a ten-year-old girl tell her own parents she was "not allowed" to tell them something? I realized immediately that the demon had threatened her in some specific way. He instructed her that it was a well-guarded secret and that if she revealed it he would do something harmful to her, her sister, or her family. It was the only thing that made sense.

Somewhere in this discussion, the father let me know that the girl had become interested in being baptized.

"Good," I said. "Tell her you can't be baptized and hold one hand up out of the water. It's all or nothing with God. If you don't get this out of her now, it could haunt her for the rest of her life."

At last report, their preacher had helped this family by meeting with the little girl and trying to get her to come clean, so to speak. Whatever the demon had threatened was causing this girl to hide something from her own parents.

As a follow-up note, I shared this story with a pastor I knew well. The next day he texted me the link to a Web site dedicated to the worship of Legba. It stated that Legba was a demon in charge of "openings, doorways, communication, and tricks." It also said he "makes things happen in all sorts of humorous, unexpected, impossible sorts of ways." It informed of his "colors": "white in Rada and red in Petro." It invited you to decorate his altar with red-and-white candles. It went on to describe specific acts of worship to Legba that involved pennies and chicken sacrifices. Let me tell you, folks: evil is real. Very real. And evil is after our children.

Lord, I praise You as the giver of dreams and solver of problems and lover of little of children. Please deliver this girl and her family from evil. Help her family and support group to have the right things to say at the right moment so this won't haunt her the rest of her life. In Jesus's name, amen.

Bible-Based Thoughts Based on This Event:

Demons can invade a Christian's own home.
Demons can sometimes target innocent children.
Demons can communicate with innocent children.
Demons can use threats to control innocent children.
Demons strategize, leaving a way, allowing their return.
Innocent children can effectively command a demon to leave.
Demons can have their communication bound through prayer.

A Shocking Miracle

Look at me and be stunned. Put your hand over your mouth in shock. (Job 21:5, NLT)

One event I was involved in near the Dallas area was quite shocking—literally.

Mary friended me on Facebook after hearing about me through a mutual friend and reading my book *My Search for Prayers Satan Hates.* They had experienced some family issues that had them concerned, so they made their own stakes and staked out their home.

A couple of months after doing that, there was a break in the city water main right in front of their home—right at the corner of their property. Work crews worked quickly to shut off the water and dig out the damaged area quickly so the water could be turned back on for the local residents.

Power-line crews had first marked off the high-voltage lines first so that the work area would be completely safe when the backhoe dug out the waterlogged area.

But they made a mistake on the location of the high-voltage line. Three workers were standing in the hole with rubber boots on and water over their ankles when the backhoe cut the power line. All three saw the wire flopping and sparking—right in the water beside them. They all jumped out quickly, stood up, and wiped themselves off. They stared at each other in amazement. They should have been dead, and they knew it. It was a miracle.

One of them was so excited about their survival that he went up to Mary's door and knocked. When Mary came to the door, the man was beside himself with excitement.

"Wanted you to know that we just had a miracle happen in your front yard," he began and then explained what had happened. "We should all be dead," he concluded as he finished the story.

Mary looked at the area where they were working and said, "Well, I know why you had a miracle there."

"Why?" he asked.

"Because we put out tent stakes with Bible verses on them on the corners of our property, and one of them is in the mud somewhere right where you guys were standing.

God is good. All the time. Count on it.

Lord, Your power is beyond measure. Grant me the faith to receive it and the courage to tell others about it—even when it seems hokey. In Jesus's name, amen.

The Atheist Teacher Next Door

> You don't believe me because you are not my sheep.
> (John 10:26, NLT)

One summer, I was scheduled to be in Chattanooga, Tennessee, for an event, so I contacted an old friend who was now preaching near that area. He invited me to come teach a Bible class to a combined adult group the Sunday morning following my Chattanooga event. It gave us a chance to catch up on our friendship, and I sold a few books and stakes to help pay for my trip. (I don't charge to speak, and when I do get an honorarium, it rarely covers just the mileage.) Soon, thereafter, they booked me to come speak at a couples' retreat.

Between presentations, one woman asked to speak to me for a moment.

"I know you're busy getting ready for the next session," she began, "but I just had to tell you this. I'm a high school science teacher. The man who teaches next door to me is an atheist. Every day after school he comes to my room and makes fun of me for being a Christian. This might include ridicule about the Bible, or even making fun of God. If I've stepped out of the classroom for a moment, he even leaves vulgar notes with insults to me or Jesus or God. So I put some of your stakes in my classroom to see what God might do. They were hidden in the corners of the room, and no one knew they were there but me. The next day after I placed them, the atheist came into my room—like he always had. But this time, it was different. He took two steps into my room and then froze. He got a funny look on his face. Then he turned and ran out. He's never been back in my room. He might yell at me from the hallway now, but he refuses to set foot inside the space protected by God's word. You're right, Steve. God's word is still powerful."

Brothers and sisters, I can't make this stuff up.

Lord, help my faith to grow. Show me what to do to help others and truly make a positive difference in their lives. And please give them faith to receive You and Your mighty works. In Jesus's name, amen.

Bible-Based Thoughts Based on This Event:

Demons attach themselves to people who then promote Satan's agenda.

Demons apparently cannot go where God's word is protecting.

Demons promote ridicule of God, His people, and His word.

The High School Counselor

You guide me with your counsel, leading me to a glorious destiny. (Ps. 73:24, NLT)

A high school counselor came up to me after one of my presentations last year. "I loved your idea of posting God's word at the workplace," she began. "My job has really gotten tough these last few years. I'm supposed to help students pick a career and a college based on their interests and aptitudes, but it has become almost impossible. Their apathetic attitudes have made that a nightmare."

"What do you mean?" I inquired.

"Well," she continued, "when they come to my office for a session, I usually begin by asking, 'What do you like? Where do your interests lie?"

They would respond, "Video games," or "Nothing," or "I don't know," as they shrugged their shoulders.

"'Great,' I would think. And the conversation would go nowhere. It was like pulling teeth to get anything constructive out of them. So I posted sticky notes all over my office with Bible verses on them—hidden in strategic places. I taped them to the back of the pictures on the wall, to the bottom of all the chairs, and underneath my desk. The idea was quickly tested when the next student arrived for a session.

"'What do you like? Where do your interests lie?' I began as usual, and their responses were completely different. They might say something like, 'I sort of like drawing,' or 'I like engineering,' etc. Then I suggest a couple of college choices that are known for those things, and they show an interest in one or two of them. Then I get the ball rolling by showing them how to request more information about applying. It's like a totally different atmosphere, and the only thing that's different is the hidden verses from the Bible that are now all over my office. You're right, Steve. God's word is still powerful."

Another home run for God. Are you surprised? I'm not—not anymore.

Lord, deliver our children from the evil one and all his forces. Put a wall of protection around them and help them in every decision. Let them feel your presence and know it's You. In Jesus's name, amen.

Bible-Based Thoughts Based on This Event:

Demons may work to make kids rebellious and focused on entertainment.

Demons may work hard to distract children from having proper focus.

Demons have less influence on children when God's word is near.

The High School Special Education Teacher

But *Jesus said, "Let the children come to me.* Don't stop them! For the Kingdom of Heaven belongs to those who are like these children." (Matt. 19:14, NLT)

One of the men in the crowd spoke up and said, *"Teacher, I brought my son so you could heal him. He is possessed by an evil spirit that won't let him talk.* And whenever this spirit seizes him, *it throws him violently to the ground. Then he foams at the mouth and grinds his teeth and becomes rigid.* So I asked your disciples to cast out the evil spirit, but they couldn't do it." *Jesus said* to them, "You faithless people! How long must I be with you? How long must I put up with you? *Bring the boy to me.*" (Mark 9:17–19, NLT)

One spring right after I spoke at the Tulsa Soul-Winning Workshop in Tulsa, Oklahoma, I got a phone call the very next week. It was from a teacher in Arkansas, who had attended my lectures and purchased some Kingdom Stakes.

"This is Mrs. Cantrell," she began. "I'm so sorry to bother you, but there's something you need to know. Do you have a minute?"

"Sure," I urged. "Tell me about it.

"Well, I'm a high school special education teacher. And I have some severely handicapped children. In fact, two of them only have an IQ of fifty. They can only count to the number four. They know some other numbers, but they can never get them in sequence. I put the stakes in the four corners of my classroom, and they both counted to one hundred. And they've done it every single day since then."

"Wow. Wow."

That's all I could think to say. My mind was spinning. If I put seventeen verses around these kids, and they counted to one hundred instead of just four. What if I put one hundred verses there? How many childhood problems and issues are demonic rather than psychosomatic?

As one of my friends put it, "Well, Jesus never came to a sick person throughout His ministry and said, 'I can't help that. It's autism,' or 'They are bipolar. Only medication can help that,' did He?" Good point! Thanks, Clint!

Lord, thank You for reminding me that You are Lord of all—all the earth, all the people, and all the diseases. No matter how mortal man has classified the problem. In Jesus's name, amen.

Bible-Based Thoughts Based on This Event:

Demons may be able to inhibit the mental capabilities of children.

Demon influence on children is diminished through displaying God's Word.

A Texas "Haunted" House

Now God worked unusual miracles by the hands of Paul, so that even handkerchiefs or aprons were brought from his body to the sick, and the diseases left them and the evil spirits went out of them. Then some of the itinerant Jewish exorcists took it upon themselves to call the name of the Lord Jesus over those who had evil spirits, saying, "We exorcise you by the Jesus whom Paul preaches." Also there were seven sons of Sceva, a Jewish chief priest, who did so. And *the evil spirit answered and said, "Jesus I know, and Paul I know; but who are you?"* Then *the man in whom the evil spirit was leaped on them, overpowered them, and prevailed* against them, so that *they fled out of that house naked and wounded.* (Acts 19:11–16, NKJV)

As I began speaking on the subject of spiritual warfare, many people began to seek me out with special questions or unique problems. Many told me stories about amazing things that had happened in the past—sometimes decades ago. They would tell me stories they had never told anyone before, fearing they would be labeled weird or crazy. Others had shared their bizarre stories with anyone who would listen. One such story involved a haunted house.

When I say *haunted*, I don't mean with spirits of the departed. I define *haunted* as demonically inhabited or harassed by demons and various kinds of evil spirits, fallen angels who followed Satan in his rebellion against God. Satan is called a dragon in Revelation, and chapter 12 verses 1–4 reveals that about one third of the angels followed him in this evil endeavor. I don't know how many that makes, but it obviously means that good angels outnumber Satan's evil horde of demons by a margin of two to one.

I want to share one of the most unique stories about a demon-possessed house from Carrol, in her own words:

In January of 1998, I married my first husband and we moved into a small pier and beam home in the country in Grimes County, Texas. I had no experience with the supernatural or spirit realm. I thought it was false and fake. I was a Christian, but I didn't think Christianity had a supernatural aspect. I thought that "spiritual occurrences" and "ghosts" were just curiosity coupled with an overactive imagination.

Not long after moving into this home, strange things begin to happen. Doors opened and shut by themselves, including being locked and unlocked. My hair dryer would come on in the middle of the night even though it wasn't plugged in. Our window unit air conditioner would come on in the middle of the night even though it wasn't plugged in. We would watch keys mysteriously move all the way across the kitchen counter when no one was even in the kitchen. We heard voices in the early morning hours and pots and pans clinking, as if there were a large feast being prepared. Through a little research, we were told two things. One, we could tell it to go in the name of Jesus. Two, that house had previously been rented by a regional member of the satanic church who was known to be a high priest.

My husband had little experience in supernatural activity, so he began trying to chase it off in the name of Jesus. As things would mysteriously begin to happen he would say, "Be gone in Jesus's name!" Unfortunately, nothing stopped. In fact when he tried to use the name of Jesus, things will only get worse.

All this made me very confused about my fate and the power of God. One night I watched my husband wrestle to open a door that was not locked. It was like there was someone on the other side holding the doorknob to keep the door from opening into the laundry room. When he finally got it open about three inches, suddenly there were three claw marks across the top of his hand and he began to bleed. Yet we saw no hand, no paw, nothing. One night, I walked into the laundry room and the window began to fog up immediately. An invisible hand began to draw a pentagram in the moisture on the window. We had had enough and knew we must leave. We began staying with my in-laws and would get clothes from the house during the daylight hours.

We did this for several weeks. If we were caught in the house after dark, things would begin to happen. One day, I was at the house by myself, and a phone call came from my grandmother. I got distracted by the phone call, and the sun dropped below the horizon before we left. By the time I hung up, grabbed my overnight bag, and started to leave the house, it was almost dark. I had left the front door wide open, but during my phone conversation, it has been closed and dead bolted. I was the only person in the home! I put my hand on the doorknob to turn it, and it was so hot that it burned the palm of my hand. At the top of my lungs, I yelled, "In Jesus's name, you will let me leave!" The door unlocked by itself and swung open, and I walked out. I did not shut the door. I did not turn around. I got in my car, and I left.

I learned a very specific lesson after this incident. I was actually trying to walk with the Lord during this time in my life. Although I stumbled, I was making an effort to live a fruitful Christian life. My husband was not. He often spoke against God and damned God with his words. He was a very angry, abusive man. When he tried to use the name of Jesus, it would not work. In fact, he would say that when he used the name of Jesus he could hear demons laughing at him. But when I used the name of Jesus to chase away those things that were threatening me, it worked! I never returned to that house after the door incident. I also learned that the power in Jesus's name is like no other. It works only for those whose faith and walk is right. You must know Jesus personally before His name can help you.

Lord, deliver me from evil. Remind me of the power of Your Name when I need it most. Help me to overcome the evil in my life and walk with You so demons run when I invoke the name of Jesus rather than laughing in my face. In Jesus's name, amen.

Bible-Based Thoughts Based on This Event:

Demons flee when hearing Jesus *uttered by a faithful Christian.*

Demons laugh when hearing Jesus *uttered by an unfaithful Christian.*

Demons can inhabit a dwelling because of the activities of the previous renter.

Demons may sometimes cause unusual occurrences in our physical realm.

Demons do their best and most terrifying work at night.

An Arkansas "Haunted" House

The Lord now *chose* seventy-two other *disciples and sent them* ahead in pairs to all the towns and places he planned to visit. Now go, and remember that I am sending you out as lambs among wolves. Whenever you enter someone's home, first say, "May God's peace be on this house." If those who live there are peaceful, the blessing will stand; if they are not, the blessing will return to you. When the seventy-two disciples returned, they joyfully reported to him, "Lord, even the *demons obey us when we use your name!*" (Luke 10:1, 3, 5, 6, 17)

I think it was a Thursday when I got the call. It was from a preacher in Arkansas. He had heard me speak on spiritual warfare, and he was now facing a problem with one of the families at his small church that he didn't quite know how to handle. He needed some expert help.

I told him I wasn't an expert, but that I would try to help. Then I asked him about the problem.

"Well," he began hesitantly, "this would sound crazy to most folks, but I think you'll understand."

Why am I the "go-to" guy for weird spiritual problems?

"Go ahead," I urged. "Nothing would surprise me anymore."

"One of the families at our church came to me with a unique problem. And they asked me to keep it completely private—to tell no one. They are afraid others will think they are crazy. I told them about your ministry, and they gave me the okay to give you a call and discuss it. They say their house is haunted."

He gave me their phone number.

I made the call. "Mrs. Smith," I began, "your preacher said you're having some strange problems at night in your house. I can come up next Tuesday if that works for you guys. And I'll spend the night in the house with you if that's okay."

She was delighted—and very thankful, not to mention relieved. Their college daughter was now refusing to be in the home after dark, and the wife retreated on some nights to a local motel. The whole family was terrified.

I met them at their church, and the entire family was there with the preacher waiting. We went into the church conference room.

After introductions all around, the minister turned the meeting over to me. I gave a quick overview about how this idea got started, sharing a few of the stories so the family would understand that this wasn't my first rodeo. My goal was to increase their faith and confidence in God. Many other families had been delivered from similar problems. This put them at ease and helped them to realize that it wasn't about me, and it wasn't about money (I had driven over five hours without any expectation of payment). God's power was their only hope.

Sometime during our discussion, they revealed that they had been contacted just prior to my arrival by a medium (a person who claims they talk to the dead) from Nebraska. This family and that medium had a mutual friend. This mutual friend had contacted the medium for advice and had ultimately given the medium their phone number. The medium had called with some wild claims:

- The medium claimed to know the "ghost" who lived in their home.
- The "ghost" was a girl named "Callie."

- "Callie" had been raped and murdered in that home.
- "Callie" loved this family's daughter, especially her jewelry and makeup.
- "Callie" would love it if they would talk out loud to her, calling her by name.

They told the medium that they were actually thinking about putting out stakes with Bible verses on them because this guy in Texas (me) was suggesting this and getting great results.

This brought a quick response from the medium. "No," she screamed all of a sudden. "Do *not* do that. That will upset the ghost," she continued. "And you don't want to upset the ghost."

Let me stop right here and make a major point: if a medium tells you *not* to do something, that's probably the exact thing you *should* do. Scripture instructs us never to consult mediums:

> "*Don't dabble in the occult or traffic with mediums; you'll pollute your souls.* I am God, your God." (Lev. 19:31, The Message)

Also, let me point out that I've used the term *ghost* in quotations because biblically there are no such things as ghosts. I think demons can disguise themselves as humans

(2 Cor. 11:14, Heb. 13:2). I believe this story about a human girl named Callie is a made-up story intended to invoke sympathy from the afflicted family. If the family realized the "ghost" was a demon, they would never consider cohabitating with it. But if they think the "ghost" is the spirit of a young, mistreated, dead girl, then they are more likely to be sympathetic as opposed to (a) leaving or (b) commanding the demon to leave in the name of Jesus.

It was getting on up in the day, and I wanted to get the stakes in around their house before dark. Satan is called the "Prince of Darkness" in Scripture, so I have made it a practice not to install them after dark (primarily because of something that happened during my stay with this family).

Their brick home sat on a lovely ten-acre pasture, and it had a carport on one end. Beyond the driveway was an old barn they were using for a storage building. I later discovered one of the spiritual issues associated with their property—civil war slaves were buried there.

It was almost dusk as we positioned the stakes just outside the four corners of their home. The husband wielded the hammer as his wife read the verses out loud at each corner. I was an agreeing witness, along with their minister.

When all four stakes were driven into the ground as far as possible, we all went into the kitchen and held hands as we prayed for peace, safety, and protection for this family. We bound and gagged any evil being associated with that property and renounced any evil or curses associated with the people or the land. Relief was visible and palpable as we ended our prayer time and got hugs all around. Their posture became totally relaxed.

After Dark

> *My enemy* has chased me. He has knocked me to the ground *and forces me to live in darkness* like those in the grave. (Ps. 143:3, NLT)

Later that evening, we sat around visiting and watching sports on television. We had been so focused on our conversation, and everything seemed so normal that it never dawned on me until about 9:30 p.m. that we were in a "haunted" house. I quickly asked, "How does tonight compare to all the evenings here in the past?"

"It's very different," they quickly responded.

"How?" I inquired.

"Well, just look at the dog," they suggested.

The dog was asleep on the floor with his head on his outstretched paws.

"The dog is just lying there asleep," I pointed out. "What's different?"

"We've never seen him this calm in the ten years we've lived here," they revealed. "He's always looking up at something in the air in the center of the room, growling," they said. "And sometimes he gets up and growls as he is looking up at an imaginary floating balloon. Nothing's there, but he follows it, growling until it stops. And then he lies down again, agitated and tense."

Animals and children often see or sense things that adults do not. I have heard stories like this from many people over the last few years.

There were many other nighttime events that they went on to describe—more than need be included for the purpose of this real-life example, but suffice it to say there were electrical appliances of various types that turned themselves on and off randomly, floating apparitions, noises, and smells that were "otherworldly" and a variety of other things. Their younger daughter, a college student, had resorted to pulling her mattress from her own bedroom to the foot of her parents' bed until she couldn't even take that anymore. She was sleeping every night at her best friend's house.

Finally, it was about 10:00 p.m. when the wife mentioned that she wanted copies of my books.

"No problem," I replied. "I'll run out to my Jeep right quick and grab some copies for you."

It never dawned on me—until it was too late—that I was about to venture out after dark beyond the perimeter of the area staked out and protected by the mighty word of God.

I stepped out of the door to their carport. There was a small light fixture with a single bulb in it, and it was a very dark night. It felt surreal, like a scene from a movie. I remember thinking the light above wasn't giving out much light, not enough, less than normal somehow. This thought passed through my mind in a millisecond, and I stepped on out—beyond the area protected by the word of God.

That's when it happened. It was the strangest feeling. It's the first time I every felt truly and completely terrified. The hair on my neck and arms stood up and prickled, a very strange sensation. And it was like someone had thrown a black, velvety blanket over my head. Blackness. Darkness. Looking back, it reminded me of the biblical description of the plague of darkness:

> Then the Lord told Moses, "Raise your hand toward the sky, and *darkness will cover the land of Egypt. It will be so dark you will be able to feel it.*" (Exod. 10:21, NCV)

The fear gripped me. I knew somehow that I wasn't alone. What did I do? I began to pray out loud for protection because the blood of Jesus covers me. I literally ran to the car, though it was only a short distance. I grabbed what I was after and ran back, and as soon as I reentered the safety zone of God's protection, the feelings of anxiety and fear went away. Relieved, I went to my room and prepared for bed.

I don't think I'll ever forget that feeling. I don't ever remember feeling so afraid. I sensed the power and anger of the enemy and the reality of the battle we face as Christians every day—whether we realize it or not.

The next morning, I was anxious to hear how everyone slept. They said they couldn't remember when they had slept so soundly. Relief was evident in the faces and attitudes of each family member.

After it was evident that what we had done made a difference, I told them about my scary visit to the Jeep the night before and how the darkness felt. The husband nodded in agreement. "I know what you mean," he started. "I had to take the dog out in the middle of the night, and as soon as I stepped outside, the hair on the back of my neck stood. I was very different outside our staked area," he finished.

The next day, I helped the family put a separate set of stakes on the corners of their ten acres and spent one last night in their home. Again I went to the Jeep for something after dark. It felt completely different. The light on the carport seemed brighter, I felt no fear, and the atmosphere felt "cleaner" than it had before.

After this unique experience, I started recommending that building and homes on larger pieces of property be staked out separately.

Castles used to have moats and walls, right? Two levels of defense can never hurt.

Lord, please choose more workers to go out and do Your work. Many are living in fear. The enemy seems to be more active than ever. Open our eyes to how we can help people get free of the spiritual bondage in homes throughout our nation and beyond. Give us the right words to make a difference. In Jesus's name, amen.

Selling a "Haunted" House

> *If the Lord doesn't build the house, the builders are working for nothing.* (Ps. 127:1, NCV)

The day this family bought this house, they drove by with excitement about their upcoming move. That's when they first noticed something strange. The seller had rented a box truck to move all his things. He had backed the truck up to the front porch and was literally running in and out of the house, throwing things in the truck haphazardly. They thought that was strange.

Then they moved in. Eventually, they understood the sentiment. In fact, they finally decided to sell the house too.

Their teenage daughter wouldn't spend the night there. The wife sometimes went to a hotel, and, although the husband refused to leave, he often felt uneasy and eerie.

It was sort of a catch-22: they couldn't talk about the strange nocturnal occurrences out of fear that folks would think they were crazy and out of fear that it would become known in the community as a "haunted house" that no one would want to buy, leaving them stuck with it. This was also a factor in their long delay for seeking help. In addition, they felt a moral obligation to "clean up" the house spiritually before selling it to someone else.

On three different occasions, they thought they had the house sold. Once the sale seemed so sure that they even moved all their furniture out. But then it fell through again, and they had no choice but to just move right back in.

When the home was finally "clean" (after my visit and the stakes and prayer help), there were just too many nightmarish memories to remain there. So they bought a new house and put the "haunted" one up for sale again. It sold rather quickly, and they felt good about "cleaning" the house up for the next owner before moving on. And as far as they know, there have been no more nighttime episodes.

God's word is still powerful.

Lord, send Your healing power throughout the land for all who have the faith to put Your word around them. In Jesus's name, amen.

As a sidenote, it was interesting to discover that there were actually quite a few abandoned, dilapidated homes in that county that no one seemed to mention or even notice anymore. It's actually a fairly common practice for people to move out of a place never to inhabit it again. Perhaps this area is especially riddled with demonic strongholds.

I actually discovered that one of my close friends had lived in that area many years ago. He described the atmosphere in that community as extremely prejudiced and ugly, with the KKK being quite active and forceful in their domination of the local government and city and county policies.

Bible-Based Thoughts Based on This Event:

Demons show up after dark; their leader (Satan) is Prince of Darkness.

Demons bank on your reluctance to seek spiritual help for nighttime occurrences.

Demons work at getting you to focus on your fears, which is most productive at night.

Demons sometimes use mediums to help create a story invoking your sympathy.

Demons use lies and sympathy to get you to become comfortable with them.

Demons do not want you to post anything connected to God on your land.

Demons serve Satan, prince of darkness, so night-time is their special time.

Demons can sometimes be quite visible to dogs and other animals.

Demons can sometimes affect electrical appliances to cause fear.

Demons can sometimes be sensed by humans in the physical realm.

Hiding God's Word Near a Loved One

Cry out for insight, and ask for understanding. Search for them as you would for silver; seek them like hidden treasures. Then you will understand what it means to fear the Lord, and you will gain knowledge of God. (Prov. 2:3–5, NLT)

One family had a daughter who had simply walked away from her faith. She finished school, moved in with a roommate, and didn't even tell her parents where she was living.

She grew more and more distant and reclusive from her family. Although she had previously talked, texted, and visited with family regularly, she now wouldn't even respond to texts from her parents saying, "I love you."

As a holiday approached, the family texted her, asking if she would come home. The response was, "No. Have to work."

But the family was praying, and prayer is powerful.

At the last minute, she texted that she would come over for a short visit.

During the visit, the family worked out a way to hide Bible verses in the girl's luggage and possessions. The visit ended, and the girl returned to her home—wherever that was.

The family continued to pray.

A short later she began to call home, wanting advice on a new career opportunity. This led to more interaction, and she started saying, "I love you," to her family again. This was a major breakthrough.

It soon became apparent that the young lady only made these emotional calls home when she was near the Bible verses. And she was totally unaware that the verses were nearby.

I really can't explain it except to say that God's word is still powerful, and prayer still works. Keep praying for your own loved ones. And if you get the chance, hide some Bible verses around them.

Lord, help me to truly believe in the power of Your word to change lives. Bless every parent who is working and praying for his or her child to return to You. In Jesus's name, amen.

Bible-Based Thoughts Based on This Event:

Demons want young people to leave their faith far behind.

Demons work to lead young people away from their family.

Prayer is still very powerful—especially from close family members.

God's word is still very powerful and can soften even the hardest heart.

Placing God's word near *a loved one is an act of faith that can make a difference.*

A Hidden Cross

> The message of *the cross* is foolish to those who are headed for destruction! But we who are being saved know it *is the very power of God.* (1 Cor. 1:18, NLT)

A long-time friend lives in a town only thirty miles away. He had just read *My Search for Prayers Satan Hates,* and it was fresh on his mind. He was sitting on his front porch, praying for his family.

His son was taking college classes while working a part-time job and still living at home. As this man prayed for his son, he had a weird feeling that he should go put a cross in his son's room. He'd never done anything like that before, and it felt quite strange, but he decided not to ignore the urge that he felt was from God since it occurred while he was praying for the boy. He retrieved a small cross from a drawer and went to boy's room to put it there. He felt so weird doing this at all that he decided to put it behind some books rather than placing it out in the open. But he did obey and put it in the boy's room. He told no one.

The next day, he went to work early without seeing his son, since the boy worked a job that ended at 11:00 p.m. at night. Later that morning, the boy showed up at his dad's office unannounced—which never happened.

"Hello, son," the father greeted him. "Come in."

The boy came in, shut the door (very unusual too), and sat down, staring at the floor. He began to cry. He cried softly at first, then sobbing and shaking, trying unsuccessfully to hold in his emotions. The dad did his best to console his son, but was at a loss since he had no clue what this was all about.

When the boy's emotions subsided a little, the concerned father asked, "Son, what's wrong?"

"I disobeyed you, Dad," the son began. "You taught me right, and I've done wrong. I need you to forgive me."

"Son," he said, "you're already forgiven. You're my son. I love you. I'll always love you—no matter what. What is it?"

"I knew it was wrong, Dad, but I did it anyway. Two girls I know started sexting me pictures, and I sexted them back pictures of me. I'm so sorry, Dad. I'm so sorry."

"It's okay, son. You are forgiven. How long has this been going on?"

"About a year."

"What made you come confess it today?"

"I don't know, Dad. When I got home from work last night, I couldn't get it off my mind. The guilt was overwhelming. I hardly slept. I knew I had to get up and come confess it to you and get right."

The only thing different in his room was the cross, hidden there behind some books the night before by the dad, at the urging of the Holy Spirit. God is good. All the time.

Lord, thank You for the power that can be seen by putting symbols of our covenant with You in strategic places. Deliver our children from evil and from the plans and schemes of the evil one against them. In Jesus's name, amen.

Bible-Based Thoughts Based on This Event:

Demons use modern technology to advance all forms of evil.

Demons focus their efforts on our children, which can usually hurt us the most.

Biblical symbols (like a cross) placed strategically can invoke conviction by the sinner.

Questions at a Drug Rehab Center

They didn't *turn away from* their murders, their spells and *drugs*, their sexual immorality, or their stealing. (Rev. 9:21, CEB)

One year, I was invited to be one of the speakers at a Prayer Workshop in North Louisiana, near West Monroe, where the Duck Commander is located.

There were several speakers on the program. I spoke Friday night, Saturday morning, and Sunday morning. The church provided lunch on Saturday for all the guests in attendance. During that meal, an older couple came up to me with a special request: "Steve," they began, "we notice you're not on the program to speak this afternoon. We lead a Bible study every Saturday at 2:00 p.m. at a drug rehab center here in town. Would you be willing to come speak to these guys today?"

"Sure." So I went with them.

We went through the procedure of adding my name to the guest list, getting a pass, and having an armed escort take us through the facility into a secure area on the second floor. A large group of guys were waiting in a large, locked room, and the guard gave us entrance for the one-hour session.

As always, I was introduced as "The Stake Guy," and I began to tell them my stories—always fun to share!

After about forty minutes, I paused (for some reason) and asked, "Does anyone have any questions?"

On my left, a hand shot up. My eyes landed on him—a big, strong guy with huge arms and a determined look on his face. I soon found out why. He had a serious question:

"I got three demons that follow me all the time. How do I get rid of them?"

That was the first question. I had never had a question like that before.

At this point, I had one thought going through my head: why in the world had I asked for questions? Wish I hadn't done that. Can you say, "Improvise"?

Asking quickly for divine guidance, I offered a solution that I need to give you some background on first.

By this point, I had gotten so many messages from people about the great things that had happened when they put the stakes in the ground around their homes and businesses that I really believed this worked. God had confirmed it so many times that even a legalistic conservative like myself had been won over. It's called faith, and I was growing in it. I had seen so many changed lives by the placing of the Kingdom Stakes that I had been brainstorming about ways to expand on this idea of displaying God's Word in various ways. One of the ladies in my small group, for example, now does embroidery of Bible verses on cup towels, which I sell to support my ministry. I also have prayer stickers to be placed on a vehicle or on a house that asks for God's protection—with scriptures at the bottom. And I also have prayer cards that are free that can be put in your pocket, in your smart phone case, or anywhere else, asking for God to put a "bubble of protection" around the person bearing it. Some parents have put them in iPad cases and seen literal personality changes in their children. (Again, I can't make this stuff up.)

When I prayed the quick prayer for wisdom about what to say to the question that day at the drug rehab facility, that prayer card came to mind. So I said to the man claiming to have three demons in his rearview mirror all the time, "Okay, God's word is powerful, right?"

"Right," he answered.

"I'm going to give you one of these prayer cards," I continued. "Put it in your billfold and keep it with you at all times, understand?"

"Yes," he agreed.

"Think of it as a bubble of protection everywhere you go, okay?"

"Okay."

"Now I'm going to pray for you," I said as I put my hand on his huge shoulder. "Dear God," I prayed, "please take away those three demons and put them in the pit. We don't want to just run them away from this man and let them hurt someone else. We bind them and gag them in the mighty name of Jesus and by His blood and command them to the pit with those disobedient angels who are there in chains, awaiting judgment (Jude 6). Amen."

As we raised our heads and our eyes met again, I said, "You won't see them anymore."

I acted like I'd done that a million times before, even though I'd never done it before.

"Any more questions?" I continued.

"I have a question." I heard the voice from the other side of the room and turned toward it.

"I'm having those nightmares you talked about. What do I do?"

"Okay," I answered, "take four of these cards just like I gave him. Put them under the four corners of your bed here at the facility. Then sit in the middle of that bed and pray for God to make that square area where you sleep a place of peace and safety in the name of Jesus. Got it?"

"Got it," he answered.

"Now I'm going to pray for you," I said as I placed my hand on his shoulder, just as I had done for the other guy a moment before.

"Lord, please take away these bad dreams in the name of Jesus. Make his bed a place of total peace. In Jesus's name, amen."

I looked up at him and added, "You won't have those bad dreams anymore."

Again, I acted like I'd done it many times before. I'd never done that in my life. I wanted him to feel confident and have faith in God's ability to deliver him and answer my prayer.

There were a few other questions, and then we left.

Four days later, I was traveling on a Wednesday night to an event in the Dallas area, about two hours from my house. My cell phone rang. As I picked it up, I noticed the face revealed that it was from Hammond, Louisiana.

I'd never heard of Hammond, Louisiana. I don't know anyone in or from Hammond, Louisiana. All this crossed my mind quickly as I answered the call.

"Hello?"

"Is this Steve Hemphill?" a female voice asked.

"Yes."

"Good!" she exclaimed. "I need you to pray for this and this and this…"

"Hold on a second," I interrupted. "Where did you get my number, and why are you asking me to pray for all this?"

"Oh," she answered, "my aunt has a grandson in a half-way house in West Monroe, Louisiana, who was having nightmares every night until you gave him those prayer cards and told him to put them under the four corners of his bed. They stopped. So I knew you were the one to call!"

"Are you a Christian?" I asked.

"Yes."

"Then you can pray. My prayers are no more powerful than yours," I explained. "It's a faith issue. Jesus couldn't do many miracles some places because the people there had no faith. See? No faith, no miracles, no answered prayers. Understand?"

"Yes," she replied, "but I still want you to pray."

I smiled.

And I prayed.

But it's not about me. It's about God.

Lord, many have been led away from you and are now subject to Satan and his demons because of drug addictions. They live in fear and terror—especially at night. Use this revelation to give them hope and courage. Deliver them. In Jesus's name, amen.

Bible-Based Thoughts Based on This Event:

Demons are sometimes visible—especially to those who've been on drugs.

Demons are actively involved in nighttime terrors, dreams, and visions.

Demons can't revisit an area that's now surrounded by God's word.

Demons can be expelled by the mighty name of Jesus Christ.

Five Demons and a Sexual Orgy

Do not have sexual relations with your brother's wife, for this would violate your brother. (Lev. 18:16, NLT)

As I've mentioned, I'm still uncomfortable sharing some of these wild stories, but I'm learning God's word is trustworthy, and I'm learning to be brave in sharing—though there will always be some Christians who doubt and even make fun of me. I can handle that too. This story and the next are even more fantastic, but I prayed about it and decided to include them, so here goes.

One spring I was invited to a workshop in Oklahoma. I also set up a small table where attendees could come ask questions and see all my resources. I had just completed an outreach series for a church in central Texas, and they had purchased several signs advertising the event to place around their city. The top headline read "Demons vs. Prayer," which is effective in bringing in community visitors. It also listed the titles of the lectures in an effort to entice visitors.

The dates of the event were listed at the bottom. Finally, it included my picture.

As a small joke, I had posted a picture of the poster of me with the church in the background with the comment, "Looking for a church to visit today. Maybe I'll go here." Many of my so-called friends began to post sarcastic and pointed comments making fun of me or simply making their own jokes. I can handle it. I learned to laugh at myself long ago. Dad always taught me that you can either laugh with others at yourself, or you can cry alone. It's your choice. One of the comments said, "If you were looking for a sign from God, I think you got it!" Funny. But I didn't realize just how prophetic that sign and that statement would become.

One of my Facebook friends is a preacher in Tennessee, and I was scheduled to help with an outreach at his church just a couple of months later. He saw the picture and sent me a message that he would like to have those signs after that church was finished with them if they didn't mind. They didn't. The preacher from Tennessee was also coming to the workshop, and he asked me to bring them to my booth there so he would stop by and pick them up.

So here I was in the booth at the workshop, and the signs were just leaning against the wall in the back of the booth behind some chairs. You could barely even see them.

A big guy came walking by in a hurry. He just nodded a quick "Hello" to me and was walking on by. But I noticed he glanced at the signs in the back of my booth on the floor, and he stopped in his tracks and walked into my booth right up to me.

"How are you?" I greeted him with a smile.

"Fine," came the response. "I need to share a couple of stories with you."

"Okay," I replied, "Let's sit in these chairs. Who told you to tell me the stories?" I questioned.

"God."

"Oh," I answered in shock, "when did He tell you that?"

"Wednesday," came the one-word response.

"Then how did you know I was the one?"

"When I saw those signs," he said as he pointed to the ones from the Texas outreach that were ready to be picked up by the preacher in Tennessee. "God said to me, 'This is the guy. Tell him.'"

The top line: "Demons vs. Prayer" was visible just above the chair backs.

"Okay," I said. "You have my attention now! I'm Steve."

"I'm Dan."

Dan went on to tell me a little about his background. He was raised in a non-Christian home in an abusive situation and was ultimately put into foster care. He was a talented football player and played for a major university.

But he had a serious injury as a freshman and never fully recovered from it, so he didn't play much. However, he was converted to Jesus during his last year in college and decided to become an outreach minister. He had worked in several states and eventually had researched and studied the topic of spiritual warfare. His fascination with the power of prayer and the evil beings mentioned throughout the Bible led him to teach a short series on Wednesday evenings to anyone interested.

At the end of the final class in the series, one couple remained to talk with him after everyone else had left.

"We have a problem, and we need your help," they began. "We have demons in our house. Can you come over?"

"I'll come tomorrow afternoon."

When he arrived at their home, the couple gave him a tour of the place. As they finished the walk-through, they were in a large family room at the back of the home. Dan looked at the room and immediately had a vision from God of what had been going on in that room.

He turned to the couple and said, "You have five demons in this house."

"That's right," they replied in shock. "How did you know that?"

"God showed me. Four of them are very big, and one is small, but the small one is the really bad one. He's the one to watch out for. He is in charge."

"That's right too! How in the world could you know that already? You just got here."

"God showed me."

"So how do we get rid of them?"

"Stop having group sex orgies in this room with other couples."

"How did you know we did that? We've never told anyone."

"As I said, God showed me."

He went on to explain how you get the Holy Spirit when you obey God and submit to baptism as a symbol of your faith.

They understood. They were baptized, and they stopped sinning sexually, and they never had another problem with demons.

Lord, help me to be pure, clean, and obedient morally. The world encourages sexual sins of all kinds, but remind me that sexual sin is not only a sin against You, but it's also a sin against my own body (1 Cor. 6:18), which will one day be resurrected. In Jesus's name, amen.

Bible-Based Thoughts Based on This Event:

Demons encourage people toward all kinds of sexual sins.

> *Demons are expelled from homes when the residents turn from sin.*
>
> *Demons have a right to be in any home that's participating in sexual sin.*

A Bedroom Demon

> Her house is the road to the grave. *Her bedroom is the den of death.* (Prov. 7:27, NLT)

Dan continued, "Here's the other story God wants me to tell you. One college girl attended that six-week class I taught on spiritual warfare. The next day after the class, she came by the church office."

"I need help," she started. "We have a demon in our house. Can you come over?"

"Yes," he answered. "I'll come after your mom gets home this evening."

The girl's mother greeted him at the door. Dan went in, and the mother-daughter duo took him to the girl's bedroom.

As soon as Dan saw the bedroom, he said God gave him another vision so he knew what to say. He said he saw the *flight path* of the demon.

"Every time the demon shows up," he said, pointing around the room, "he comes in the door right here. He goes up, across here, and lands over there on that shelf. That's where he stays."

"That's exactly right," the girl answered. "How did you know that?"

"God showed me."

"How do we get rid of it?" the mother asked.

Dan turned to the mom. "Your daughter needs to stop having sex in here with her cousin," he said in a very matter-of-factly manner.

"My daughter would never do that," she said, appalled.

"I'm so sorry, Mom," they both heard the girl say.

———✦———

Demon problem solved.

Lord, open our eyes to how sexual sin opens us up to the demonic, making Satan our master instead of You. Deliver us from this obsession. In Jesus's name, amen.

Bible-Based Thoughts Based on This Event:

Demons often target college-aged kids toward sexual sins.

> *Sexual sin can sometimes bring demons into view.*
> *Sexual sin invites the demonic into your home.*

Bugs in the Night

> *It came to me in a disturbing vision at night*, when people are in a deep sleep. (Job 4:13, NLT)

It's very common when I start an outreach at a church to begin on Sunday morning and kick things off by having a potluck luncheon where all the visitors are invited to stay and visit. This was the case at one Texas church, and one of the deacons told me that a visitor needed to talk to me. That's when I met Michael.

Michael had recently been released from jail. He had been a mule who delivered drugs from dealers to users. Once out, his old employers immediately contacted him. They wanted him back. And the money was good. He agonized about it because he needed the cash badly but ultimately said no to their offer on account of his grandson.

Michael just had one daughter, and she just had the one child. The infant was only six months old but was already the pride and joy of Michael's life. As Michael had struggled with his decision about employment, he realized that if he got caught again and went back to jail, he would be leaving his grandson and his daughter high and dry. They couldn't make it without him. Once he gave them his final answer (no), bad things started happening in his house at night. Really bad, really scary things. It was almost as if someone had put a curse on him...

Michael lived about twenty miles out in the country, and the newspaper advertisement he saw talking about "Demons vs. Prayer" got his attention because he had just started dealing with "issues" in the night, and he felt that it had to be demonic. When I heard his story, I couldn't disagree.

"I need help," he began frantically. His voice was stressed, as was his whole demeanor. "I can't get anyone to come to my house and help me. Can you come help me? Please?"

"What's wrong with your house?" I asked.

"Bugs," came the quick reply. "Lots and lots of bugs in the night. They only show up at night. I can't get rid of them. I've tried everything. I've been spending over a hundred dollars a month on cleaners and bug poison, but nothing works. I've even mixed bleach with the poisons, but that didn't help either, and I burned my hands from the chemical mix I put together. Please come help me. Will you come?" he asked in desperation.

"I'll be there as soon as I can this afternoon. I need to stay until this is over. Then I'll change clothes and drive out in the country to your house."

I got directions. It was about twenty miles out.

When I arrived at his house, he was waiting for me outside, wringing his hands in fear and anticipation.

"Thank you so much for coming," he began. "My cousin promised me she would come pray, but then she prayed for someone in the hospital with a skin disease, and she got the same disease, so she changed her mind and refused to help."

I'm just telling you what he said. I can't make this stuff up.

"Are you a Christian?"

"No," he answered, "but I've thought about it."

"Is this your property?" I asked.

"Yes."

I held a hammer and the four stakes for the corners of his lot.

"Do you have a camera phone?" I inquired.

"Yes."

"Good," I said. "Take a picture of the verses listed on these stakes. I want you to read them out loud later in your house."

He got the camera focused and made a picture of each stake, making sure the verses listed were readable.

"Okay," I encouraged. "You are the authority over this property. You are going to be the one to put the stakes in the corners. I'm in agreement with you, I'm a witness for you, and I'll pray with you when we're done."

"Okay."

We began. He hammered a stake deep into the ground at each corner of his property. We talked as we walked. I was trying to encourage him. The frantic desperation was almost palpable—you could just about taste it in the air.

As we did the deed and as we talked and visited, there was a noticeable change in his demeanor. He went from talking fast to talking much slower. He went from an attitude of fear to a relaxed, almost calm approach. He listened to everything I said. I reminded him that God was powerful and that God has spoken the words that were now posted on the corners of his property. It was like a wall of protection. He openly admitted that he felt better.

"That's good," I encouraged. "But I do need to warn you."

"About what?" he quizzed, a little fear creeping back into his voice.

"You're clean right now, but you're still vulnerable."

"What do you mean?" he said with growing concern.

"There's a story in the Bible about someone who got rid of a demon but didn't fill themselves with God. That demon went and got seven more demons to come back with him to live in the same man again. So that man was much worse off in the end with a new total of eight demons inside when he previously had only one (not that it's okay to have any).

He nodded his head in silence. I could tell the idea was sinking in. Now it was time for the remedy for that.

"Do you have a Bible?" I inquired.

"Yes," he said, "New King James."

"Go get it," I instructed.

He opened it, and we read some of the verses together. He had trouble finding some of the books, so I pointed out the index in the front that gave him the page numbers. Again, he relaxed as we did this.

"Open up Acts chapter 2," I asked, "and read verse 38 out loud." He did:

> And Peter answered them, *Repent* (change your views and purpose to accept the will of God in your inner selves instead of rejecting it) *and be baptized*, every one of you, in the name of Jesus Christ *for* the *forgiveness* of and release *from your sins; and you shall receive the gift of the Holy Spirit.* (Acts 2:38, AMP)

"What does that teach?" I asked him.

"That we need to repent and be baptized for the forgiveness of our sins and then we get the Holy Spirit."

"Bingo," I replied enthusiastically. "The Holy Spirit is the defense you need against this evil enemy who is out to get you. Understand?"

"Yes. I think so," he said as he contemplated that thought.

"Okay," I went on. "I need to go. I preach again in a little while, and I need to change clothes and eat supper first. I'm a diabetic, and I need to eat before I speak. I hope you'll come."

"I'll be there," he stated flatly.

I drove away and hoped he would.

The singing ended, and it was my time to get up and present my second lesson in a series of five. Here are the titles I usually like to cover in a lecture series:

1. Spiritual War in a Physical World
2. Satan's Tackle Box and Prayers He Hates
3. Following God through Tough Times and Great Difficulty
4. Demonic Harassment Today and Prayer Hindrances
5. Thinking like the Enemy

It was Sunday night. I had just gotten started when Michael and his daughter walked in the door to sit down. The daughter's boyfriend, an ex-marine, was carrying Michael's grandchild—a six-month-old baby boy. They sat about halfway down toward the front. I welcomed Michael by name from the pulpit. I was very glad to see him there. He smiled like a happy child. I think it made him feel important.

I thought about Michael all through the lesson, and every time I glanced his way, I noticed that he was paying close attention. As I was winding down and making my last point, I thought about Michael again. I offered an invitation for anyone who needed to respond to the gospel:

"We're going to have an invitation song now," I instructed, "and anyone who needs to can come forward."

I looked right at Michael and said, "Somebody..."—I smiled—"might...want to be baptized." He smiled back. I knew he was with me.

He came forward during that song, and I had the privilege of baptizing him. The joy on his face was radiant.

After the service, I found myself out in the lobby. Many were huddled around Michael, hugging and congratulating him; others were asking me questions about demons, nightmares, and prayers to fight that.

David—the ex-marine who was dating Michael's daughter—came right up beside me and stated in a sullen, almost angry voice, "I need to talk to you." He gritted his teeth, and I saw his jaw clench, waiting for my answer.

"Let's step off over to the side right here," I suggested as I moved to the side of the foyer, where everyone was gathering. It wasn't all that private, but we could talk softly and be fine.

"I was in Iraq," he started. "I was shot right here," he added as he pointed to the center of his chest, "and I've seen things no one should have to see. I want you to know something. The Bible don't mean *nothin'* to me." He stared at me in defiance, daring me to contradict him.

I think he was quite surprised with my response.

I began nodded in agreement, saying, "That makes perfect sense to me."

"It does?"

"Yep. In fact, I can show you a Bible verse that says if you're not a Christian, you're not a spiritual man and you won't understand things of the Spirit of God. Only Christians will understand that."

> But *people who aren't spiritual can't receive these truths from God's Spirit.* It all sounds foolish to them and they can't understand it, *for only those who are spiritual can understand what the Spirit means.* (1 Cor. 2:14, NLT)

"Really?" he said weakly. All the power was gone from his tone and attitude. He was truly puzzled at my answer.

"Really," I confirmed. "But I can change that if you'll let me. Can I pray for you right now?" I asked.

He nodded with a soft, "Okay."

He was a lot bigger than I was, so I reached up and put my hand on his shoulder and began: "Dear God," I started, "David doesn't think you love him. I pray You'll lead him to open a Bible and, wherever he reads, he will be able to see how much You love him. In Jesus's name, amen."

I met his gaze with complete confidence: "Let me know how that works out for you, David, okay?"

I walked away, feeling God's release on that situation.

I found out the next day that a veteran from the Viet-Nam Conflict overheard that whole conversation. He went up to David and said, "We need to talk."

See how God works? David had a new friend with much in common because of that simple little prayer.

I don't know the end of David's story, but I plan to look him up in heaven and hear it.

Back to Michael:

All Michael's nighttime "episodes" stopped after staking out his house. He was so relieved. He texted me daily to express his heartfelt thanks.

Then one day he called, adding some additional information: "Last night, it started to happen again," he began, "so I did just what you said: I took out my Bible and began walking around the house reading the verses that are on the stakes. It stopped. You're right, Steve," he concluded. "God's word is powerful.

About two months went by before I heard from Michael again. It was a Saturday morning, and it was a rare weekend at home with nothing to do. His number is programmed into my phone, so I knew who it was when I picked it up and answered, "Hello, Michael! How are you?"

"Okay," came the weak answer. "Everything's okay…"

"What is it, Michael? Something's wrong?"

"No," he replied, "everything's really okay…Nothing's going on at night…It's just that …something happened last night, and when I woke up this morning, God said, 'Call Steve Hemphill.'"

"Michael, what happened last night?"

"Well…I met this woman…and…everything's okay… but we talked until late…and it was so late that I ended up staying there all night…and…ahhh…"

"You had sex with her, didn't you, Michael?"

"Yes," he admitted.

"Michael," I informed him, "you just gave Satan the right to come back into your house."

Michael started crying. Sobbing.

I waited for it to subside a little and then interrupted. "It's okay, Michael. It can be fixed. You need to confess it and repent and pray, and God will forgive you and protect you again, understand? You can't display symbols around your home of your covenant with God and then not live by the covenant. It's called sexual sin, and it separates you from God's protection and provision, understand?"

"Yes," he replied.

We prayed on the phone together.

"Michael," I went on, "you need other people to be praying for you besides just me—people to support you on a weekly basis. You don't have to confess the details at church, but it might be good for you to go forward at an invitation and ask for prayers because you are struggling in your Christian walk. Got it?"

"Got it," he said. And he did.

I still hear from Michael every now and then. A quick text or a short phone call. It's always the same thing—appreciation for helping him escape from a deep, dark place that no one should have to experience. I always notice the joy in his voice as he describes his beautiful grandson. God delivers. From anything. And He also restores your joy. Remember that. Remember Michael.

Lord, thank You for touching Michael's heart and his life with Your wonderful truths. Thank You for sending him to that little church outreach where we could connect. And thank You for delivering him from the hand of evil beings—both the visible ones who were selling drugs and the invisible ones who were attacking him at night. In Jesus's name, amen.

Bible-Based Thoughts Based on This Event:

Demonic manifestations are designed to cause fear in the heart of their target.

Demons can manifest as bugs in the darkness—or as a hallucination of such.

Demons can be associated with curses on those who refuse to help them.

Demons can't touch those who repent and return to God after sin.

Red Eyes

When it sneezes, it flashes light! *Its eyes are like the red of dawn.* (Job 41:18, NLT)

As I just described, Michael's grandson means the world to him. And that is very understandable. One of the reasons it's so special to Michael is because of something Michael saw in his grandson's eyes before I met him. Let me explain why this caught my attention.

As people have come to me with story after story, I have noticed several recurring themes. One of these has to do with red eyes. When people see a dark figure at night, red eyes are what they mention most often. I've also begun to notice this in the writings of other authors who have written on the subject of demons.

One of these books is Michael Leehan's book *Ascent from Darkness*. Michael and I are friends now, and he's now a Christian author and speaker who literally speaks all over the world. But he grew up in a difficult home. At a young age, he decided God didn't love him, so he decided to serve Satan. And serve Satan he did—for over twenty years. He claims his primary assignment was to attend Christian churches and pretend to be a Christian so he could infiltrate the enemy camp and cause strife and dissension. He prayed satanic curses on people and things to help his cause. He was even baptized at one point—not because he believed in Jesus—but in order to convince the enemy he was on their side so they'd let their guard down. It was a very effective strategy. I highly recommend the book, but it's not for the faint of heart or for a new Christian. Only seasoned believers can handle the details revealed in its covers. A movie about his experience is being filmed called *The Adversary*.

Leehan is one of many I have personally talked to about the red eyes he saw at night. Demons are often described as having red eyes by eyewitness accounts.

I was reminded of this one day when this Michael saw his innocent little grandson's eyes turn red one day. It caused him to scream in panic, "No. Not my little one!"

He says he thinks about that day often, and it makes him even more grateful for our friendship and how our connection led him to God and Jesus and the safety he now enjoys in his home. God is good. All the time.

Lord, protect the little children. Don't let the enemy have them. Surround them with Your mighty angels and keep them safe from all harm. In Jesus's name, amen.

Bible-Based Thoughts Based on This Event:

Demons can sometimes cause you to see scary visions.

Demons are often described as having piercing red eyes.

Demons want you to fear that they control your loved ones.

Bed Bugs at Night

You will not fear any danger by night or an arrow during the day. (Ps. 91:5, NCV)

A church friend called me one day—a widow lady from a Bible class I teach on Wednesday nights when I'm in town. "My friend Frank wants to talk to you. He's worried he has a generational curse. I told him that you had been teaching on spiritual warfare, and he wants to meet you."

I got his phone number and gave him a call. He wanted to meet for breakfast and talk face-to-face. I'm an early riser, so that suits me just fine.

We met at IHOP. I don't eat much breakfast, but I love their coffee, and I ordered a pancake. If I ate every day what I saw Frank eat, I'd weigh over three hundred pounds in no time. But he worked a hard schedule, and he wasn't fat at all.

"What makes you think you have a generational curse?" I inquired.

"Well," he explained, "my grandfather was bipolar, and my mom is bipolar, and I'm worried I'm starting to have some symptoms of being bipolar too."

"Don't focus on that," I urged. "Focus on God and His promises. Satan uses fear and tries to get us to worry about things like that for one reason only: fear displaces faith. You can't be full of fear and full of faith at the same time, understand?"

"I think so," he answered.

"Are you going to church?" I asked.

"No. I used to, but there are so many hypocrites."

"I understand—and I sympathize. But remember, we're all hypocrites at some time or another."

"You know what Satan's looking for?" I asked him.

"What?"

"He's looking for sheep who aren't with the other sheep."

A look of understanding dawned slowly across the features of his face.

"Not going to church because of hypocrites is like not going to the gym because there are lots of fat people there. Fat people are the ones who need the gym."

He smiled. That thought penetrated his defenses too.

"One more thought on that. And I'm not telling you what to do. I'm just giving you some ideas to consider, okay?"

"Okay."

"I got to thinking about all that one day because I hear lots of folks today saying, 'I love Jesus, but I hate organized religion.' But that's like saying, 'I love you, but I absolutely hate your wife.' How would that make me feel? Bad, right? On top of that, I found several verses that said, 'As was his custom, Jesus went to the synagogue on the Sabbath.' Who was Jesus going to church with? He was going to church with the very people planning His murder. If anyone had a valid excuse to not go to church because of all the hypocrites, it was Jesus. But he didn't do that. He went anyway. And He's our example. Understand?"

"I understand," he responded with resolve.

"If you'll go to church, not only will you be blessed, you'll also be a blessing to others. It's a two-way street. You benefit, and so do others. God ordained the church, and going is important. Find some place you can be comfortable, because you need it. More than you know."

I also explained living by your covenant with God. "Covenant people get covenant blessings over and over," I told him. "You'll be surprised how many blessings will come your way because of your friendship with church people—if you'll be faithful."

That's come true over and over. He's called me many times to tell me that.

God is good.

One of his less-than-stellar relationships was with a woman who came to his home one day.

"We didn't do any real bad things," he explained gingerly. "But we did some things we shouldn't have been doing. And after that, I had bedbugs in my house."

"Let me know if that changes when you stake your place out with the Kingdom Stakes," I requested.

He did. No more bedbugs.

God is good. All the time.

Lord, help me to focus on my faith so my fears will evaporate. Remind me that those two cannot coexist. Lead me to grow in my faith so I can serve You better and live a life of joy and kingdom promotion every day as Your ambassador. In Jesus's name, amen.

Bible-Based Thoughts Based on This Event:

Demons definitely discourage folks from church attendance.

Demons can manifest themselves as bugs in certain situations.

Demons work hard to instill fear in their victims so faith cannot grow.

Demons can promote generational sin and worry through fear and intimidation.

Angels Descending

After all *this I saw another angel come down from heaven with great authority*, and the earth grew bright with his splendor. (Rev. 18:1, NLT)

One of the things I've begun to notice is that people who have had issues with drug addictions—prescription or otherwise—often have the ability to see things and beings that others cannot see. This theory holds true for a friend of mine named Janet.

Janet is a preacher's wife. She lives about forty-five minutes away, and her husband is pastor of a nondenominational church. Janet has a rare blood disease, which has required the use of strong pain medicine over the years, and that's where the problem began. Ultimately, she was addicted to a prescription and had to attend a drug rehab program. Imagine a preacher's wife in a facility with a variety of gang members and homeless people who share the same problem chemically. Difficult, to say the least.

During this time in her life, Janet heard a "voice" that was continually telling her that she was no good, her husband would never want her back, and her life was over so she might as well end it and put everyone out of their misery. (See how Satan uses a progression to help inflate the suicide numbers?) Note: Janet's entire story is now in a book called *Set Free*.

But Janet obeyed another voice instead—the voice of God.

I mention all this in the context that people like Janet commonly sees into the unseen dimension on occasion. And Janet's revelation one afternoon that was connected to the Kingdom Stakes helped me understand why they were working so well when put out as an act of faith in the one and only God. Let me explain.

Janet is now the director of a women's shelter in her town. John, another friend of mine, is the director of the men's shelter. Janet and John heard about my stakes and drove to Longview to get two sets—one set to put around the women's shelter and another for the men's.

First they placed a set around the women's shelter. Everything was normal. Then they drove to the newly purchased property nearby that was about to have some portable buildings installed and become the men's shelter.

John had the hammer and stakes; Janet was there for moral support, as a witness, and to agree with him in a final prayer after the installation.

They had walked the perimeter of the lot, and three stakes were already in the ground. John was carrying the hammer and the final stake. There were some high weeds, so John was walking in front, with Janet following in his wake. All of a sudden, John heard Janet gasp in amazement and say, "Oh my goodness."

John swung around quickly, "What is it?" he inquired, fearing it was a snake or spider or something similar that lives in weedy areas like that, but he saw that Janet was looking up into the sky with her hand over her mouth.

"Do you see that?" asked Janet, not taking her eyes off the sky, her head moving slightly as if following a moving object.

John looked up too, quickly scanning the horizon in all directions so as not to miss anything. "No. I don't see anything. What is it?" he asked again.

Janet spoke softly and reverently, almost as if she was in shock. She was watching angels descend from heaven. There were four of them. There was one for each stake. And they were huge. Very huge.

Later, when John asked for more details, she explained to him that each angel descended to the surface of the land—then below the surface. They sunk into the dirt up to their waist. They were facing outward, the lot for the shelter at their back, as if watching diligently for enemies of any kind. They had on a gold breastplate like shining armor. It had a beautiful design sketched into the gold, like a repeating pattern that might have a deeper meaning.

Then she gave some details about their wings. By huge, she meant really, extremely huge. The stakes were about a hundred feet apart, and each angel's wings could reach the next stake. That means they had about a two-hundred-foot wing span. And each wing stayed spread, the tips tucking into the ground just below the adjacent stakes, like a fence protecting the property. And since each angel's wing tucked under another stake where a comrade angel was stationed, that meant a double fence bordered each side of the property with a double-wing formation. Awesome. They were focused and alert, though she couldn't really make out their faces. She saw big bodies and huge frames with bulging muscles.

As John and Janet told me about this soon after it happened, I just had one thing to say:

"If that's what's happening in the unseen when people place these Kingdom Stakes in the seen, it's no wonder it works so well."

Amen?

Therefore, *angels are only servants—spirits sent to care for people who will inherit salvation.* (Heb. 1:14, NLT)

Lord, thank You for creating angels as ministering serving those who will be saved. In Jesus's name, amen.

Bible-Based Thoughts Based on This Event:

Angels may be dispatched to guard land areas staked out for God.

Angels are mighty and focused mighty and alert mighty, diligent, and mighty.

Did I mention mighty?

Hand Washing

(The Pharisees and all the *Jews never eat before washing their hands in the way required by their unwritten laws.* And when they buy something in the market, they never eat it until they wash themselves in a special way. They also follow many other unwritten laws, such as the washing of cups, pitchers, and pots.) *The Pharisees and the teachers of the law said to Jesus, "Why don't your followers obey the unwritten laws which have been handed down to us? Why do your*

followers eat their food with hands that are not clean?"
(Mark 7:3–5, NCV)

Another very interesting tidbit revealing some details about subtle instances of spiritual warfare in the Scriptures has to do with this verse from Mark 7. I read this in a book, then confirmed it with my own research. It was explained in a Jewish Encyclopedia published in the early 1900s.

Pharisees in this passage are seen attacking Jesus about not washing their hands before eating. In our modern times, we'd focus on this as an unwise practice just for sanitary reasons. The Jews seem to focus on it being wrong from a tradition standpoint. But there's something even deeper—speaking from a spiritual standpoint.

When I read it, he had my full attention—since I'd never hear of it before, so I researched it on the Internet. And although many commentaries and study guides ignore Mark 7:3–5 completely, some referred to what Perry said about it vaguely, and then I discovered that some ancient Jewish encyclopedias refer to it (the 1906 Jewish Encyclopedia is one of them).

The Jewish thinkers and religious leaders of that time thought that evil had full reign after dark. They did their worst during the nighttime hours. So the ritual of hand-washing in the morning before eating—and especially before prayer—was one that cleansed the person from the demons that got on them during the night. They believed that a spirit of impurity attaches itself to each person during the night because the soul temporarily leaves the body while the person is asleep, leaving them vulnerable to evil spirits. They even specify that you should have a water basin within four yards of the bed so you can rid yourself of them as quickly as possible after awakening.

Truth is stranger than fiction, isn't it?

> This is the message we have heard from him and declare to you: *God is light; in him there is no darkness at all.* (1 John 1:5, NIV)

Lord, I praise You as the Light. No darkness is in You at all. Your adversary—Satan, prince of darkness—is also my adversary. Deliver me from him all the time, but especially at night. In Jesus's name, amen.

The Evolution of the Stake

> The tree grew very tall and strong, reaching high into the heavens for all the world to see. (Dan. 4:11, NLT)

The story of how the Kingdom Stakes started is something I will never forget. People getting results, people calling wanting to buy stakes, me refusing to sell them—telling them to make their own. Then getting talked into selling stakes, then selling lots more stakes than books. I still can't believe it as I look back.

My men's small group started hearing all the stories of people wanting to buy stakes and then all the questions people had when I told them to make their own:

- Did you make them or buy them?
- What did you make them out of?
- Where did you buy them?
- Metal or plastic?
- How many do you put out?
- How far apart are they?
- How deep are they?
- One verse on each one?
- Multiple verses on each one?
- How many verses on each one?
- Do you leave them visible?
- How deep are they?
- Can I put them on my vehicle?
- Should I put them in my suitcase for trips?
- Can I use them in motel rooms?

And on and on it went. It literally became comical—but it wasn't. Why? Because people's lives were literally changed over and over for the better. I can't make this stuff up.

It started small. I ordered fifty. Then I had to order more and more often so I quickly changed it to one hundred, then two hundred, and then three hundred at a time.

I was ordering them from a camping company in New Jersey (because I'm a tightwad, and they were the cheapest—even with the freight cost). They finally called me one day and said, "Sir, we can't keep up with the number of stakes you're buying. You're going to have to find another vendor."

"Really? Okay."

I googled for a place to buy large quantities of a simple, nine-inch tent stake. I found a company that bid on large quantities of single items—like stakes—and filled out their bid request form on line. They called in less than thirty minutes. The price was a little cheaper than I'd been paying. "I'll take three hundred," I told them, and they arrived four days later.

But people called or came by and bought or ordered from my Web site at PrayerThoughts.com, and I actually sold half of them the day after came in. I called back: "Give me six hundred more," I requested.

"Sir," they responded, "what are you doing with all these stakes? You've ordered nine hundred stakes in less than two weeks. And you don't want any tents with these stakes?"

"No tents," I replied. "The apostle Paul handled the tents. I just do the stakes that go with them." Then I explained the stories and what they were being used for.

"That's awesome, sir," they said. "We're going to expedite your orders so you get them very quickly each time you call."

"Great."

Next thing you know, I'm getting a call from a plastics manufacturer in Northeast Texas—Jacksonville, to be exact.

"Steve, I hear you're buying lots of stakes and putting Bible verses on them."

"That's right."

"We can make those for you right here in East Texas. We've been in business since 1968, and we can even design the mold so the verses are part of the mold. When they pop out of the mold, they won't need any stickers—all the verses will be on every single stake!"

"Wow," I replied, "that would be great! How does this work?" I asked.

"You buy the mold, and then we make the stakes for you."

"I knew there was a catch. How much is a mold?"

"Never mind that for a minute," the guy said. "Why are you doing this? What are you doing with all these stakes?"

I started telling him the stories. After a few minutes, he interrupted.

"Okay. I want to hear all your stories. You can tell them to me when you come to the plant for a tour. Right now, let's talk about the stakes. We can design them with two rows of verses on each side…"

"Hold on." I interrupted. "I don't want to waste your time. I need to know how much the molds are if I have to buy that because I'm sure it's not cheap, and I can't afford thousands of dollars."

"Well," he replied slowly and thoughtfully, "molds usually cost around ten thousand dollars. But don't worry about that…I'll pay for that."

"What?" I demanded? "What do you mean?"

"This is obviously a God-Thing," he answered, "and I want to help with it. I'll pay for the mold. You just pay me what you're already paying for stakes."

God is good. All the time. Praise the name of God.

Lord, I praise Your name as the One and Only God and King of the universe. And every time someone puts Kingdom Stakes around their property, remind them that since You made the world. It's Yours, and as Your children, we have the right to stake it out for You. In Jesus's name, amen.

Stakes and Realtors

> Ask of me, and *I will make* the nations your heritage, and *the ends of the earth your possession.* (Ps. 2:8, esv)

As I finished assembling the stories for this book, a strange, exciting, new phenomenon began to occur. Let me explain, because it might be something you would like to put together for your church in your hometown.

As I have stated, Satan has taken the land. He has put his best warriors in Washington, DC, and Hollywood, California, and that's been a very effective strategy. I say let's mark it off—house by house—and take it back for God. Are you with me?

In that vein, I had some local realtors who had been buying stakes from me when one of the houses they had listed wouldn't sell. They would put out stakes, pray for God's protection and intervention, and then when potential buyers looked at the property, it was like they were seeing it with brand-new eyes. Every nook and cranny looked cozy rather than cramped. Every room looked efficient rather than small. And every style looked uniquely attractive rather than weird. It's hard to explain; it just worked. It's all about God. When His word is invoked, it never comes back empty-handed:

> So shall *My word* be that *goes forth* from My mouth; *it shall not return to Me void, but it shall accomplish what I please, and it shall prosper in the thing for which I sent it.* (Isa. 55:11, NKJV)

I am on the road speaking a lot lately, but when I'm home, I attend a terrific small group. Most of our group is noticeably older than me and my wife, but we really feel a closeness to these folks—salt-of-the-earth kind of people. They are always anxious to hear how my last trip went and all the new stories I have to share. I love seeing the smiles on their faces as I recount the mighty things God did for people on my last excursion.

At one of our small group Bible study sessions, we decided to brainstorm some ways we might could use the Kingdom Stakes as an outreach and get more people in Longview to stake out their land for God—from huge farms to small lots. The crime rate here has soared the last few years, and we're anxious to see it fall as more and more people invoke the name of the Lord God in our county. We are sure things will improve.

This is what we came up with: We would offer free stakes to the realtors (I would sell them at a discount to our group. I don't get a salary for doing ministry. They wanted to help me). Then the realtors would offer them to the families who are selling their property as a "thank you" gift. That way, there were no legal issues. Then the stakes would be installed (hidden deep in the ground at the corners). Once the house sells, the realtor would let us know the address and name of the buyer so we could deliver a framed prayer that looks like this:

> Lord, please put Your angels around this family and this property and provide divine protection for all who enter here. In the mighty name of Jesus. Amen.
>
> Genesis 1:1, 2 Samuel 22:3, Psalm 7:1, 10, Luke 4:10, Ezra 8:21-22, John 17:11, Nehemiah 4:9, Revelation 3:10, Job 1:10, Job 11:18, Proverbs 30:5, Isaiah 33:21, Jeremiah 1:8, Matthew 26:53, Mark 6:20, Acts 26:22, 1Peter 1:5
>
> PrayerThoughts.com

Isn't that a great idea! The framed prayer would be accompanied by a welcome packet. There are several critical moments in life—moments when people are more likely to accept an invitation to visit a new church (yours). One is when you're married, another is when you have a child, and the last is when you move. I invite you to try this. See what God will do in your life, your family, your church, your community, your city, your state, your nation, and the world. No use thinking small, right?

Lord, use this idea to bless people and families and churches and communities and counties and states and nations all over the world to Your glory. In Jesus's name, amen.

APPENDIX A

The Original Stake Story

THE ORIGINAL STORY of how I came up with the idea of staking out the land for God is in a previous book, *My Search for Prayers Satan Hates*; but since it's the basis for all these subsequent events and stories in this book, it bears repeating here. Refer to that book if you need more detail.

Note: all names have been changed.

Larry called, asking for help with a friend who thought he had demonic activity on his business property. He was so frightened that he was even unwilling to go on the property in broad daylight unless I went with him.

Bill and Larry had been friends for years. Bill blamed God for the untimely death of his son. In addition, Bill's business was failing, his employees had betrayed him, and the economy had taken a dive.

Larry picked me up at ten that next morning, and we headed out for our appointment with Bill. We had printed Bible verses, a sledgehammer, and four stakes.

It was cold and windy on Saturday morning. Larry and I pulled up into a grocery store parking lot to meet Bill. It was only a block from the property, but Bill wasn't about to go there by himself.

Bill got out of his truck and got in the car with us. The first thing he said was, "I'm this close to suicide."

Bill did not commit suicide. The things we did over the next few minutes changed his whole perspective—and mine.

We drove up to the one-story brick building. I got out and said, "Oh my goodness."

"What?" Bill asked as he got out and slammed the door.

"Look around," I said.

"What do you mean?" he questioned.

"This property is business poison," I replied. Almost everything it touches is out of business. Behind it was an old, empty nursing home. To the right was an abandoned used-car lot. The offices across the street all had "For Rent" signs in the window. The only active business close was an auto-parts store, and it was obviously struggling. Saturday is when all the shade tree mechanics are buying parts, and there was only one car there. It belonged to the man running the register.

"I know the man who owns that chain," I told Bill. "He has thirty-two stores, and I can tell you this one isn't doing so hot. The other thirty-one are carrying it."

"Wait here," I instructed.

I walked the perimeter, praying as I went. I hadn't planned that. It was a spontaneous decision. It took several minutes since it was quite a large lot.

I silently asked God all the way around for wisdom, discernment, and for anything evil to be removed in the name of Jesus Christ and by His authority—not mine. I was so focused on my petitions. Larry and Bill were focused on me.

When I was back around, Bill came over quickly. "What did you just do?" he asked. "Something changed—I felt it."

"Not much," I answered. "I just prayed.

Bill stared and said, "The prayer of a righteous man availeth much..."

He knew the verse.

The three of us walked toward the first corner, a grassy knoll with a stop sign on a hump. Without even thinking, I said, "Bill, the first one will be the hardest." I don't even know why I said it; it came out before I thought.

Bill is a big guy with powerful arms. It's a small grassy knoll, and he has a sledgehammer. Bill knelt and began tapping the stake. He got it to stand on its own and began to hit harder and harder. It went in about halfway and stopped.

Bill was putting the full force of his weight into every blow, but it wasn't cooperating.

I began to panic. I thought, *Oh no, I've put God's name on the line, and he's hit a rock.* Before I realized it, I put my hand on Bill's shoulder and said, "You're doing great, Bill. Let me help you finish this one."

He was hitting it so hard that the stop sign was trembling with every blow, but the stake wasn't going anywhere. He looked up at me like I was crazy because he was twice my size. But he stood up and handed me the sledge.

I dropped to my knees, raised the hammer, and prayed for help.

I did hit it hard, and it did take a few blows, but I got it to ground level and then sunk it lower. I stood up hurriedly and headed toward the next corner like it was no problem at all, like I did this all the time; and it was to be expected. But inside I was relieved and shocked, and I didn't want Bill to see the shock on my face.

Behind me I heard Bill say, "How did you do that? I was hitting it way harder than you."

"Don't worry about that," I responded without thinking. "It's a spiritual thing. The next one will be easier," I instructed.

The next spot certainly should have been easier.

It was out in a grassy yard that covered the area sloping up to an abandoned nursing home. Bill knelt and placed the second stake. The process repeated itself except that this time it went about three-quarters of the way in. But it was sticking up enough that a mower would definitely hit it. Bill was on his knees, giving it all he had—again.

Again I spoke up, "Let me help you, Bill. You are doing great, but I'll have to finish this one for you too."

By now he was a believer, so he handed the sledge right over.

I bend down with a little more confidence this time, thinking that God got me through the first one. He can do it again. With only a few quick blows, it sunk down deep. No mower would ever hit it.

Again I arose and heard admiring desperation in Bill's voice, "How are you doing this? I'm hitting it much harder than you."

And again, before I could think, I responded, "Don't worry about it, Bill. You'll get the next one."

He did. He struggled a little, but he got the third stake in.

"This last one will be the easiest." Why did I say that?

He gave me that how-do-you-know look. But when we got to the last spot, I wished I hadn't said it. It was on the highway, and it was solid asphalt. You never know what's under it.

But Bill looked confident now. He positioned the stake and pounded away. It went in easily.

"How did you know that would be easy?"

"I don't know. I just knew."

After this, everything in Bill's life changed. It was like the scales fell from his eyes. He read the Bible and prayed and understood what he was reading. The next week, Bill and his wife dedicated their lives to Christ and were baptized.

> Peter replied, "Each of you must repent of your sins and turn to God, and *be baptized* in the name of Jesus Christ for the forgiveness of your sins. *Then you will receive* the gift of *the Holy Spirit*." (Acts 2:38, NLT)

Now Bill and his wife had the protection of the Holy Spirit, which is exactly what you need to protect you against the enemy who is out to get you like a roaring lion.

Lord, bless Bill and his family as they walk through life. Let their witness help lead many people to Jesus Christ and a life of safety from all the evil demons in the unseen realm. In Jesus's name, amen.

Bible-Based Thoughts Based on This Event:

Demons can either live on a particular piece of land or at least visit often (nightly?).

> *Demons work to get you to focus on ways you have been hurt or mistreated.*

Demons can work to cause your business to decline or fail completely.

Demons encourage humans to betray each other and cause heartache.

Demon departure can sometimes be sensed by the parties involved.

Demons can work to prevent stakes with Bible verses from being installed.

Demons are defeated and expelled by the Word of God being planted in faith.

APPENDIX B

Markers on the Land Scriptural Examples

> Then the Lord appeared to Abram and said, "I will
> give this land to your descendants." And *Abram
> built an altar there* and dedicated it to the Lord, who
> had appeared to him. (Gen. 12:7, NLT)

UP UNTIL MY experience with Bill and the stakes, I had
never noticed that God's people put markers on the land
throughout the Bible. The list that follows is not meant to
be exhaustive, but simply informative. Once you start to
notice this phenomenon, you'll find yourself seeing it in
many unexpected places in the Bible.

Tombstones: We still do tombstones today, and it's a very
old tradition. Genesis 35:20 reveals that Jacob set up a
stone monument over Rachel's grave.

Lord, I look forward to the day when the tombs will be opened and all the dead will live again. May that day come soon. In Jesus's name, amen.

Circumcision: Genesis 17:13 calls circumcision the sign of an everlasting covenant. God literally put a mark on His people.

Lord, I praise You as the God who loves His people enough to mark each and every one. In Jesus's name, amen.

Jacob and Laban: After gathering a pile of stones to commemorate the event, Jacob sat down with his father-in-law for a covenant meal. The stones marked the spot of this momentous event (Gen. 31:46).

Lord, thank You for the things that remind us of your involvement in our lives—whether we are asleep or awake. In Jesus's name, amen.

Altar of Uncut Stones: Deuteronomy 27:6 is just one scripture where it's revealed that Abraham built an altar to God on the land God promised him. It looks like he built more than one. Genesis 12:7, 13:18, and 22:9 are examples.

Lord, may my life be an altar of uncut stones that bring You great glory. Remind me that I'm an ambassador for You and that others are watching how I react to the events in my daily life. In Jesus's name, amen.

Jacob's Dream: Jacob dreamed of a ladder connecting the seen with the unseen. This dream is mentioned in Genesis

28:12, and angels were using the ladder for two-way transportation. Verse 18 is quite interesting, as Jacob takes the actual stone he had laid his head on for a pillow when the dream had filled his mind. The stone was a literal memorial for the spot, and Jacob even used that spot to make a vow to God (Gen. 31:13). Jacob's dream motivated him to make an eternal vow of commitment to the Lord God.

Lord, if You decide to communicate to me in a dream, help me to recognize it and understand it. Your ways are above my ways. In Jesus's name, amen.

Anointing Jacob's Stone: Another unique "marking" used throughout the Bible is anointing oil. Genesis 28:18 also reveals olive oil as a marker on an object—making it holy to the Lord. (This procedure appears later in the New Testament in connection with healings and demonic exorcisms.)

Lord, anoint my heart and my life with Your special oil. Mark me as Yours. Lead me each step of the way and help me to honor You with every thought, every word, and every deed. In Jesus's name, amen.

Goshen in Egypt: Exodus 8:22 in the ESV states flatly that Goshen—the part of Egypt where Israel lived—was set apart. Notice that the plagues didn't affect Goshen like it did the rest of Egypt.

Lord, I want to live in a land protected by You. In Jesus's name, amen.

Blood Marked the Doorpost: Definitely one the most famous marks in the Bible was the blood on the doorpost (Exod. 12:13). Literal blood was to be smeared on the doorframe of the house of each and every Jew. This blood was a like a neon sign telling the death angel (probably a demon, since the last enemy Jesus plans to defeat is death) to hit the road. The firstborn son of each blood-marked house was to be left alone. Obedience to God by each individual family saved their firstborn sons.

Lord, let my house be a home covered in the blood of the Lamb—a place of peace and safety and rest for all who enter. Use my property, my life, and my talents to bring glory to Your name and Your Kingdom. In Jesus's name, amen.

The Tabernacle: As I mentioned, oil was used throughout Scripture to mark what was holy and dedicated to serving God. The anointing of the Tabernacle in Exodus 40:9 is one of the earliest examples of this.

Lord, anoint me with Your holy oil, and mark me as Your own. Show me what to do for Your Kingdom today. In Jesus's name, amen.

Marking Sets Apart: Verse 13 of Exodus 40 goes on to indicate that an anointing set someone apart for a position of special service to God—dedicated to His purposes.

The Priests: Anointing oil placed on Aaron's head made him holy and ready to serve God in a special way (Lev. 8:12).

The Sacrifices: Exodus 40:10 also implies that the anointing of the sacrifices for God made them absolutely holy.

Lord, I know You created me to serve You in some special way. Just as no two snowflakes are alike, no two humans are exactly like. Help me to find and fulfill my purpose for You. In Jesus's name, amen.

Generational Marks: Exodus 40:15 advances this idea even further, indicating that some assignments are generational—being passed down like a covenant or a blessing from father to son and beyond.

Lord, I pray that the marks you put on my life will carry over to my children, grandchildren, and all the generations to come—until You come! In Jesus's name, amen.

Mount Sinai: Moses was instructed in Exodus 19:11–12 to set limits around Mount Sinai. What sort of limits? It doesn't say. But one thing's for sure: it wasn't an invisible or imaginary line. It was something real and practical and visible—like piles of rocks or stakes.

Lord, mark the boarders of my home and deliver me from the evil that abounds in the world around me today. I can only survive with Your supernatural and angelic protection. In Jesus's name, amen.

The Jordan River: There's a very unique placement of rocks in Joshua 4:9. When Israel crossed the Jordan River—at flood stage so God could demonstrate His power—the priests were standing in the middle of the dry riverbed as the people passed by them into the Promised Land. God had instructed him to get rocks from the riverbed and carry them to their camp to pile them up as a memorial, reminding them of God's power and greatness, but he also took it upon himself to put an additional twelve stones—one for each tribe—in the middle of the riverbed and put them in the exact spot where the priests had held the ark.

Lord, help me to have the faith to pick up my life and cross the places that look uncrossable. Remind me that You can do anything. Your power overcomes all others. In Jesus's name, amen.

Markers Mean Something: Israel crossed the Jordan River into Canaan. God instructed Joshua to pile up twelve stones where they crossed as a memorial—a monument designed to cause their children to ask questions. This was to give families the opportunity to tell the story of God's powerful hand in their daily lives facing real problems (Josh. 4:21). A modern version of this would be baptism or the Lord's Supper.

Lord, help me as I tell my children the greatness of Your power and Your abilities. Let my words about You to them inspire them to follow You and obey Your every command during their lifetime on earth. Help them to be an inspiration to others. In Jesus's name, amen.

The Israelite Campsite: An additional detail is given in Joshua 4:1–3 about the twelve stones they carried from the dry riverbed: it marked their campsite. Their camp was where they slept, ate, fellowshipped, and wanted to hear from God about their next move. It was a place to rest, plan strategy against their enemies, and be with family. The campsite was their temporary home. Today, our homes, farms, and apartments are our temporary homes; heaven is our permanent one—our own Promised Land.

Lord, please make my campsite—my house—a place that honors You in every possible way. Help me remember that this home is temporary, but the one You are building for me in eternity is everlasting. Help me to live every day in light of eternity. In Jesus's name, amen.

The Blessing—a Land Promise: During Jacob's dream of the stairway to heaven, God promised to give him the literal ground He was lying on (Gen. 28:13). God didn't mean all land everywhere; there were limits. Other verses spell out the exact locations, but the point here is that God meant a designated area.

The Borders of Each Tribe: Ezekiel 48:29 says that every tribe had a specific allotted area they possessed, farmed, and passed on to their descendants.

Temple Land: The land set aside for the Temple and worship was also specifically marked off and dedicated to God (Ezek. 48:8).

Cities of Refuge: Deuteronomy 4:41 mentions three cities that were marked off and set aside as cities of refuge.

Moses specified these as refuge cities for issues like accidentally killing someone, preventing their own death in light of the eye-for-an-eye and life-for-life law.

Lord, forgive me for wanting to expand my own domain beyond what You wanted me to have. Help me to be satisfied with Your promises and Your provision. Help me to operate within the area You have set out for me to have authority over. Remind me that my success in one area of life doesn't automatically mean You will bless everything I choose to do—especially if I haven't consulted You before moving forward. I need Your help in every single decision, Lord, every single day. In Jesus's name, amen.

Kings Were Anointed: All the kings of Israel were marked for God with olive oil by the hand of a prophet. Samuel anointed Saul in 1 Samuel 10:1, and David in 1 Samuel 16:13, and Zadok anointed Solomon in 1 Kings 1:39. This symbolic act set them apart as holy and dedicated to serving God in a special position.

Lord, forgive me for putting my kingdom above Yours in many of my past decisions. From now on, help me to put Your agenda above mine. Help me to be willing to change my schedule for what You place in front of me to do. In Jesus's name, amen.

Territorial Authority of Angels: Jude just has one chapter, and verse 6 reveals that angelic authorities were placed by God in positions of authority on earth in the unseen. Some of those angels overstepped their bounds, angering God.

Lord, help me to never overstep the boundaries of authority You designed me. Help me to accomplish everything You created me to accomplish—not one thing more because that would be prideful, and not one thing less because that would be wasteful. In Jesus's name, amen.

Marking All Godly People: Psalm 4:3 is just one of many places discussing God's practice of setting the godly apart for Himself—for His personal, eternal agenda. Circumcision was a literal mark used in the Old Testament mentioned earlier, and, interestingly enough, Colossians 2:11–12 says that baptism is spiritual circumcision. So God is still marking His people. Jeremiah 1:5 reveals another sweet detail: God set the godly apart before they were even born. Acts 20:32 adds that the godly who have been set apart will receive a unique inheritance. Acts 26:18 informs us that faith is the ingredient necessary to be a person marked—set apart—for the Lord.

Lord, I'm willing to submit to whatever You command. Don't let me be deceived by human thought or human wisdom. Help me to have the faith I need to move forward in confidence instead of fear. Remind me that You always take care of Your own. I'm on a mission for You, and nothing can stop me from completing my kingdom work. In Jesus's name, amen.

Jesus Was Marked: In John 10:36, Jesus declares that God set him apart to be sent to earth. In Matthew 28:18, He reveals that the Father gave Him all authority, and Hebrews

2:8 adds that absolutely nothing was left out of that declaration. Psalm 118:22 is one of many scriptures calling Jesus Christ the cornerstone of the church. Remember, a cornerstone is a marker. Isaiah 28:16 calls Jesus a safe cornerstone—a safe foundation on which to build your life. I also found it fascinating that the NLT version of Zechariah 10:4 calls Jesus our "tent peg." John 19:18 says they nailed Jesus to a cross, so he took those nail prints as marks on His own body for us. Luke 24:40–41 describes Jesus after His resurrection with the marks (nail prints) on his body still visible.

Lord, thank You for taking the marks of the cross on Your own body—just for me.

Binding and Loosing: Once you have become a Christian—declaring your faith publically and entering the waters of baptism as a public display of your desire to die to self and live for Christ's agenda—Matthew 16:19 says that whatever we bind in the seen will be bound in the unseen and whatever we loose in the seen will be loosed in the unseen. When we forgive in the seen, it truly makes a difference on the spiritual condition of both the forgiver and the forgive-ee. When we command in the seen that demons be bound and gagged, that's exactly what happens in the unseen. (So get to it.)

Lord, deliver me from unforgiveness and bitterness. Help me to see others through Your eyes. And remind me that I have access to Your power when the enemy tries to overwhelm me. May my responses bring great glory to Your Name. Also, Lord, please help me to understand the spiritual implications of this binding and loosing. Help me understand how what I bind in the seen by praying is actually bound in the unseen (like demons). Help me to use this tool of power in a way that frees the prisoners and encourages the depressed. In Jesus's name, amen.